WORK IS THERAPY

The History of the
Birmingham Industrial Therapy Association
1963 – 2003

WORK IS THERAPY

The History of the
Birmingham Industrial Therapy Association
1963 – 2003

Dr. Norman Imlah

BREWIN BOOKS

First published by
Brewin Books Ltd, 56 Alcester Road,
Studley, Warwickshire B80 7LG in 2003.
www.brewinbooks.com

ISBN 1 85858 247 4

A Cataloguing in Publication Record
for this title is available from the British Library.

Typeset in Times
Made & Printed in Great Britain.

Contents

Acknowledgements

To the founders of the industrial therapy movement.

To the consultants, nursing staff and management at All Saints Hospital who believed in the value of rehabilitation and supported the development of BITA.

To my fellow Directors for their sage advice, support and encouragement over the years.

To Ron Keeling, former student and current IT tutor at Warwick Training Centre for his time, effort, skill and persistence in transcribing my handwritten text from manuscript into printed copy.

To Marie Taylor for her kind loan of photographs used in this publication.

To my publishers Brewin Books for their expert advice and encouragement.

To our current Chief Executive Erica Barnett for the contribution of her chapter and her encouragement in producing this book.

To my wife Hazel, for putting up with 40 years of archive material being strewn around the house for the last year, and for her unfailing support.

Foreword

Sadly, there is still a stigma with regard to mental illness. A physical illness can be seen in some way, whether through an injury or through the symptoms of a disease, and thus it encourages a sympathetic response; but because mental illness does not show itself in a physical manner then it leads many people to regard the mentally ill in a negative way. This negativity is made worse by ill-founded beliefs that those who are mentally ill are somehow weaker than others, that they are swinging the lead and that they need to pull themselves together. But in truth, there but for the Grace of God go I.

If we are truthful, at some stage how many of us have been close to a nervous breakdown and/or depression. I know I have. When I was on the dole I felt I had lost my manhood, that my dignity had been stripped from me and that my pride had been stolen from me. I felt less than worthless. I felt that I was worth nothing. Thankfully I was helped by my wife, mother and father, brother and other close relatives and but for their support perhaps I may have been unable to learn to deal with my deep feelings of anger, hurt, shame and alienation.

There are many people who do not have such support and who suffer from the prejudice of society against the mentally ill. If that prejudice is to be challenged and overcome then as responsible and caring citizens we need to be educated about mental illness. We need to understand the people who are mentally ill and we need to learn to be as sympathetic and supportive to them as we can be. And we need to learn to do that in a way that is not patronising or disempowering. Above all we need to learn that the mentally ill should not be stigmatised as somehow alien, for we too can become mentally ill. That is why this book is so important. The work of a distinguished doctor, it brings to the fore the History of the Birmingham Industrial Therapy Association and through that it educates us about mental illness. A pioneering body that seeks to enable social rehabilitation and to allow independent employment, it is now the only industrial therapy unit in the country.

The task of overcoming the ghettoisation of our fellows who are mentally ill is a difficult and demanding one. Thanks to Dr Norman Imlah and his associates that task may be made a little easier through an awareness of the history of the Birmingham Industrial Therapy Unit and a raising up of our knowledge, understanding and sympathy of the mentally ill.

Professor Carl Chinn MBE

'To all the many individuals - patients, clients, service users - whatever their designation at different times, who passed through the doors of BITA during the past 40 years and hopefully, benefited from the experience.'

Chapter One

HISTORICAL BACKGROUND

By the middle of the twentieth century the predominant care of the seriously mentally ill was contained, within Britain, in a large number of institutions, built mainly during the latter half of the nineteenth century. Over the years the majority of the population of these institutions, originally designated asylums, became permanent inhabitants. Some became permanent from the first admission, others from a second or third admission. A minority had a serious illness from which they had a full remission or had several admissions with remissions and relapses.

Well over half the permanent population of the institutions were diagnosed as having a form of an illness which came to be generally known as schizophrenia. Even today there is no clear agreement on whether schizophrenia is a single entity or a group of related illnesses. Whatever the differences in presentation the fate of the great majority was to occupy the long stay wards of the asylums with the prefix label of "Chronic".

Even by 1950 there seemed little prospect of this situation undergoing radical change. Despite attempts to treat schizophrenia by various methods, in particular from the nineteen thirties onwards, by insulin therapy, convulsive drugs, electro-shock therapy and brain surgery, the best that was achieved in the majority of cases was some temporary remission. Even before the advent of these treatments, there had been many approaches based on theories of causation which have been discarded. In Birmingham, between the wars, the theory of causation by focal sepsis was promoted vigorously, and ended with many patients losing their tonsils, teeth, appendices and other potential sources of infection, but still remained in the asylum with their illnesses unremitted.

Some serious illnesses did respond to new treatments. Some types of depression responded to electro-convulsive therapy, and psychotic illnesses brought on by the late effect of venereal disease, began to disappear after the advent of Penicillin killed the primary infection. Nevertheless, the post-war population of the asylums rose steadily and by the early nineteen fifties all of them were seriously overcrowded. This rise was not an indication of a rise in the incidence of serious mental illness, but was predominantly brought about by the improvements in treatment of physical illnesses through antibiotics. Tuberculosis was a constant problem in large institutions and most asylums had their own sanatorium or provision made within a group of hospitals where one would care for the considerable number of patients who developed tuberculosis. In addition, outbreaks of other chest infections and intestinal infections played their part in keeping population numbers down. Once these conditions were largely eliminated as causes of death, the numbers and the ages of the mental hospital populations began to rise steadily with no corresponding levels of therapeutic improvement for the mental disorders.

From the outset there was a widespread recognition by the doctors and nurses in the asylums that work was therapeutic; that it did not cure any illnesses, but was beneficial by giving interest, meaning and a measure of fulfilment. If one reads the annual reports of many of these institutions there are references in the earliest of these reports to the benefits of work. The first medical superintendent of the Birmingham City Lunatic Asylum (latterly All Saints Hospital) refers regularly to the therapeutic benefits of meaningful activity, both work and recreational.

Work for the inmates took a number of forms, depending upon any special skills, and relative stabilities. Many became regular employees in the various hospital departments such as kitchens, gardens, carpenter's shop, upholsterer's shop and all the various other departments which existed within the virtually self-contained communities. In the process they contributed significantly to the economy of the establishment. Payments were generally in the form of pocket money, in kind (usually cigarettes) or by special privileges, such as having their own ward key. Others less skilled, but still capable of working daily were put into squads which kept the grounds tidy, cleaned the wards and corridors or more prestigiously worked in the hospital farm. Many asylums ran their own farms with a farm manager and a squad of selected inmates, usually supervised by one or two attendants whose own background had been in farming. These farms were major contributors to food supplies in the asylum and the labour cost very little. However, there were still large numbers of the asylum population who were either too disturbed by the effects of their illness, or too apathetic after years of being locked away that they neither worked or played.

In the nineteen fifties, new and hitherto unforeseen means of treating schizophrenia changed this situation quite rapidly. It was preceded by the introduction of the National Health Service when all the asylums were taken over, and soon designated mental hospitals. Initially, most major mental hospitals had their own management committees, many of them run by a quite different type of person, with a different philosophy of care. The prevailing influence in the early days of the NHS came from the political left, deeply committed to the socialist ideology of "total care from the cradle to the grave".

In the six years between the advent of the NHS and the introduction of new ways of treating schizophrenia there was a change in attitude to patient workers. As the, then innocent, belief prevailed that the state would provide everything, the pressure to shore up the economy by patient labour was lessened, although in many hospital departments it continued. One of the early casualties were the hospital farms. It was said at All Saints Hospital that the decision to dispose of its farm, taken over with the hospital in 1948, came when the new management committee were informed that the prize bull, for which they had paid a considerable sum, was found to be infertile, and without offspring. The realisation that fecundity could not be purchased concentrated the minds of the committee that as managers of farms they were out of their depth.

For this, and different but analogous reasons, by 1954 a lot of the traditional occupations in the old asylum had disappeared along with the name. In 1954, two drugs, independently researched, were found, by chance, to produce remarkable improvements in the treatment of schizophrenia. One of these, Reserpine, did not survive for long because of it's side-effects, but the other, Chlorpromazine was the first of a range of drugs, initially called major tranquillisers, or neuroleptics, which are still the mainstay of treatment today. Despite their enormous significance they do not actually cure schizophrenia, and although they have been improved upon in various ways in the near fifty years since their introduction, there is still no true cure for this most destructive of illnesses.

The introduction of the drugs did however transform the course of the illness, and with it the whole ethos of the mental health hospital changed. Disturbed behaviour was greatly reduced and destructive symptoms eliminated or suppressed. It became evident that many previously seriously disturbed patients were now well enough to leave hospital and re-enter society.

It was from this background that industrial therapy units developed. Improved treatment, overcrowded mental hospitals and a lack of facilities to observe and acquire work skills led to the setting up of workshops and factories in many hospitals in Britain. As early as 1955 a survey of industrial therapy units in Europe was reported in the Lancet. The authors envisaged the mental hospital of the future as "a school for social learning where the psychotic, discarded by society as a whole" would acquire the social and work skills to return to the community or live at an enhanced level within the hospital.

Although the majority of the units in Britain started inside the mental hospital and many continued thus, for some the ideal position was to take the industrial unit outside the hospital. The pioneer in this development was Dr. Donal Early, Medical Superintendent of Glenside Hospital, Bristol who in 1960 formed a private company, The Industrial Therapy Organisation (Bristol) Ltd. Its objects were to provide a gradient of employment from projects in hospitals through more complex training at the factory, to independent employment, and combining with it social rehabilitation, preparing the long stay patient to resume ordinary life outside the hospital.

From these beginnings industrial therapy in Britain developed along independent and haphazard paths. No firm national policy was laid down, and it was left very much in the hands of local hospitals, and individuals in those hospitals, to develop the process. Many chose to continue their industrial therapy within the hospital, many providing a mixture of an industrial type unit in the hospital, traditional occupational therapy and domestic and other duties within the departments of the hospital. These hospital based units varied in size, and in the way they were run. Some hospitals ran the units with their nursing or occupational therapy staff whilst some employed supervisors with an industrial background to manage the hospital unit.

However, in different areas of the country, the Bristol model of an organisation providing training for work and social skills within the community was the preferred option. For the most part, like the hospital based industrial workshops, they sub-contracted work from local industry, reflecting the work that might be available to the rehabilitee. Some concentrated on marketing their own goods notably Cheadle Royal Industries Ltd in Manchester where three quarters of their production concentrated on the manufacture and marketing of paper carnival goods, rosettes, cake frills etc. Most developed a mixture of sub-contracted local industry and production of own products with, in most cases, more emphasis on the former because it was easier to develop and readily available.

It was against this background that the Birmingham Industrial Therapy Association was formed in 1963 and subsequently developed. It was not the first, but in its intent and constitution it took the first, at Bristol, as its model. It was therefore one of the early pioneers of this type of approach and a major contributor to the retraining of people leaving hospitals, many after many years, and returning them to the community, able to take their place in that community. Like all the others, it developed over the years, its own distinctive approach, an approach which has had to be periodically re-evaluated and restructured to meet ever-changing patterns of care and economic changes.

Today most of the old asylums, or mental hospitals as they became, are closed, and with their closure, their industrial therapy units. The various industrial therapy associations have disappeared also over the years, with one exception, the Birmingham Industrial Therapy Association.

It is about to celebrate the fortieth anniversary of its formation. As the sole survivor of those pioneers it seems an appropriate time to tell the story of its formation and subsequent history.

Chapter Two

BEGINNING

I decided to relate the formation and early history of the Birmingham Industrial Therapy Association in the first person as the sole survivor of those initially involved in its birth, because some is anecdotal and depends upon recollection of events, although most of it is from personal documents and from early records and reports.

I became Medical Director of All Saints Hospital, Birmingham on 1st January 1964. Like most of the hospitals in the country, and all of the Birmingham hospitals, it was seriously overcrowded. In All Saints there were 1200 inpatients in accommodation that could comfortably only accommodate 600. It was made clear at the time of my appointment that tackling the overcrowding was a top priority.

Not only was the main hospital and its annexes seriously overcrowded in the long stay areas, but there were two long-stay complexes, one at Glenthorn in Erdington and one at Uffculme in Moseley, which the Regional Board were anxious to close. It was evident from the outset that ways had to be found to return a significant proportion of the long-stay hospital population to the community, but at the same time they should not be cast willy-nilly into the outside world, as was to happen later in the nineteen eighties and early nineties with the residue of the mental hospital long-stay population, without adequate preparation of both the patient and the community. On the credit side many of the long-stay population of the mid-sixties had work skills and quiescent illnesses and no longer required detention in hospital.

All Saints, like many other hospitals, had already had an industrial therapy workshop by 1964, and there was a very considerable amount of effort in providing hospital-based work and training, but it had not led to any significant shift in the long-stay population. It was as an initial attempt to change this situation that my predecessor, Doctor James O'Reilly met with two friends to discuss the possibility of setting up some community based work project, in 1962, that led to the formation of the Association. He met with Mr. W.W. Kirk, a local industrialist, who was chairman of the Birmingham Association for Mental Health, and Mr. Bernard Davis, the head of a firm of accountants, a member of a Hospital Management Committee, and well known for his involvement in charitable work. The outcome of these deliberations was the suggestion that a car wash be developed in the city, outside the hospital, with a group of patients providing a hand car wash service under supervision.

The Hospital Management Committee were persuaded to support this venture and an Association based on the Bristol model was formed. The Birmingham Industrial Therapy Association was incorporated on the 1st day of February 1963, as a company limited by guarantee, and not having a share capital. The directors were a combination of psychiatrists, businessmen and representatives of hospital management.

The Articles of the Association stressed three main objectives:

1. *To assist in the treatment and care of persons who shall be under treatment for, or recovering from psychiatric illness of any description.*
2. *The provision of facilities for work and recreation as may be suited to them, whereby they may regain their health and prepare themselves for resuming normal living.*
3. *To sell their services, or the produce of their labour, for which they will be paid.*

My involvement with the Association began in 1963 some weeks before taking up my appointment. Dr. O'Reilly was due to retire at the end of 1963, and the other directors of the new association did not consider that they should proceed with their plans unless his successor supported them. The plans that existed were to proceed with a community-based car wash. Mr. Kirk and Mr. Davis had offered an interest free loan of £3000 for equipment and materials, and a site in Northbrook Street, just off the mainstream Dudley Road, had been obtained through the Chairman of Public Works on Birmingham City Council at a nominal rental. The site was scheduled for housing development at a future date. The hospital had already begun a car washing scheme within the hospital grounds, run by the hospital management as part of the internal industrial workshops.

While I had, at that stage, no firm views on how work rehabilitation should be organised, the car wash, in itself seemed a modest enough venture and there was no reason to object to the plans proceeding. It was further agreed that I should take Dr. O'Reilly's place as a director of the Association when I succeeded him at the hospital.

Much of the preparatory work on the site was carried out by patients from the hospital. Car washing began in January 1964, the effective operational beginning of the Association. An average of fifteen patients were employed under a charge nurse and an assistant nurse seconded from the hospital.

From the beginning it proved a successful and profitable exercise. By 1965 the average number of cars washed weekly was 375, and by 1968 this average had increased to 396. The peak number of cars in a single week was 641. Profits ranging from £50 and £100 per week allowed the original loan to be repaid, after which the profits became available to the Association to fund further rehabilitative developments.

It became necessary for me, during my first year as Medical Director of All Saints, to advise and direct our policy towards rehabilitation and resettlement in the community. It was soon apparent to me that as far as training for employment was concerned the hospital-based workshop was not the answer. Together with some of the other directors visits were made to several industrial units to get ideas about the best way forward, having seen the limitations of the hospital units. It was clear that maintenance of a busy atmosphere was essential with the emphasis on creating an authentic working environment involving the realities of working life such as daily travel, arriving on time, meeting production targets and meaningful activity. Only in these ways could the returning patient be assessed on their capacity to sustain outside employment or be trained up to the necessary standard.

Within the hospital-based workshop the ability to travel to work and arrive on time could not be tested. The pace of the hospital workshop was too slow and institutionally oriented to judge ability to sustain work at a required level, and the supervision in the workshops was still mainly that of carers whose instincts were to protect, and not to push to the limits that would be demanded by supervisors in the workplace.

It was considerations of this kind that led to my belief that it was necessary to take the main rehabilitative workshops outside All Saints Hospital and set them up in the community in an, as far as possible, authentic working environment. However I was anxious also at that time to avoid a situation, such as that in Epsom, where an otherwise excellent I.T.O. had virtually no hospital involvement. It seemed at the time that the ideal was to create something midway between the two extremes of the hospital unit run entirely by hospital personnel, and the community I.R.U. run entirely separately from the hospital. In effect an organisation that was representative of all sides, but with an independence of its own.

Having made the decision to expand from a car wash to a full industrial factory replacing the main hospital-based industrial unit, it was first necessary to persuade the hospital management committee. The concept was discussed and fully supported by the business-based directors of the Association, of whom Mr. Kirk and Mr. Davis were the dominant forces. The concept was also supported by senior medical and nursing staff in the hospital and its passage through the management committee was greatly aided by two important changes in the management of the Association.

When the Association was formed the Chairman of the All Saints Management Committee was Mr. W. Haynes who became, by virtue of his position, a founder director. Soon after the Association began its car wash operation Mr. Haynes became president of his Trade Union, moved to London and resigned in consequence from the H.M.C. and the Association. His replacement as Chairman of All Saints management Committee was Mr. H.H. Cohen who was a school dentist with a long history of public service, a former member of the ill-fated

Rubery/Hollymoor H.M.C., from which he had emerged with great credit. From almost the outset of his appointment Mr. Cohen became convinced of the objectives of the Association, and took the place of Mr. Haynes as a director.

Mr. Cohen did not think his role as Chairman of the H.M.C. was compatible with chairing the Association and doubted whether his background equipped him for this role. The directors of the Association decided that ideally they should look for somebody who combined an involvement in the health service with a knowledge of industry and industrial relations and after a good deal of discussion decided to approach Mr. J. Glyn Picton to become Chairman of the Association before embarking on its expansion.

Mr. Picton was the vice chairman of the Birmingham Regional Hospital Board. He was also Senior Lecturer in the Faculty of Commerce and Social Science at Birmingham University. Because of his expertise in industrial relations, he had become a national figure after his appointment by the government to arbitrate in industrial disputes, most notably a strike in South Wales. Due to his background of knowledge of industry and commerce, and his close connections within the local Regional Hospital Board and the Ministry of Labour he appeared to be an ideal choice, and proved to be. The directors of the Association were delighted when he accepted their invitation. Mr. Picton continued to Chair the Board of Directors for many years until ill health caused his sudden retirement, after which I succeeded him as Chairman. However, at the time of his appointment to the Chair, my fellow Directors considered that because of my role in the hospital, it would be appropriate to combine this with the position of Managing Director of the Association. At the time there seemed to be a logical argument for combining the two roles and I agreed, anticipating it to be a role that could be relinquished once the Association was well established. In fact, such were the demands that the role was not given up until we appointed a Chief Executive for the first time in 1996.

With our management structure thus in place we proceeded through negotiation from an organisation running one car wash to opening our first factory at 75 Heaton Street, Hockley on 29th November 1965. It was a disused former banjo making factory in an area due for redevelopment, and like the car wash site was leased to us by the City Council on the recommendation of the Public Works Department at a peppercorn rental. It was never intended to be a permanent site from the outset, but it was a beginning and served the initial purpose of transferring the main industrial workshop from the hospital to the community.

Chapter Three

EARLY DAYS: HEATON STREET
AND VINCENT PARADE

Despite all round agreement, the transfer to Heaton Street did not go entirely smoothly. There were last minute objections from the hospital secretary, perhaps understandable at the time. Mental hospital financing was kept on a very tight budget with little money left over for innovation. The development of industrial therapy units within hospitals gave finance officers extra revenue, as profits were made despite the fact that the big winners were the firms sub-contracting as work was taken on at a ridiculously low rate simply to provide the work. Nevertheless the amount paid to the patient worker was severely limited by law so both the firms sub-contracting and the hospital secretaries were happy. One of the first things the outside industrial therapy units did was to negotiate more realistic payments for work, but even then the rate was inevitably low.

Objections to the sub-contracted work being transferred from the hospital authorities to the Association resulted from this blow to the financial administration of the hospital, but when it was pointed out by me that the patient labour would be withdrawn from the hospital workshop in any case, on therapeutic principles, the last objections were overcome. Additionally the Birmingham Regional Hospital Board which allocated finance to the individual H.M.C.s was fully supportive of the move, and remained a firm supporter of the Association throughout its existence.

The Heaton Street factory, in Hockley was a twenty minute walk from All Saints Hospital and during our time there was attended only by patients from that hospital, and although places were on offer to other hospitals it was too inconveniently situated for the other city hospitals to take up the offer.

By 1st March 1966 there were 120 patients from the hospital in regular attendance. When the initial move was made it was done with the transfer of the supervisory nursing staff who had been working within the hospital workshops, an arrangement which was to continue after negotiation with the hospital management for some years. However the Association began to recruit its own staff to administer day to day running. Those initial staff numbered four: a secretary-bookkeeper, a driver, a representative to liaise with commercial firms for suitable work and a general manager.

The appointment of the first general manager provoked a lot of discussion because there was no accepted qualification for such a post. Eventually we made a somewhat unexpected appointment by offering the post, at the suggestion of Mr. Kirk, to Alderman Denis Thomas. For seven years he had chaired the Public Works Committee of the City Council, during the period of much development such as the Rotunda, the Horsefair roundabout and the Bull Ring, now disappearing under new development. In his position at Public Works he had been instrumental in finding the site for the car wash, and the disused Heaton Street factory. Before his civic duties occupied him full time he had been a toolmaker and a social worker. Fortuitively the control of the City Council changed hands leaving Alderman Thomas without immediate employment. It was evident that his appointment would be a short-term solution but he did remain general manager until April 1968 when he took up a directorship with Barmatic. Apart from anything else, his political contacts and knowledge of the city and its institutions were invaluable in the early years, and he used his knowledge and contacts when we moved from Heaton Street to a much larger and centrally placed old factory at 78 Vincent Parade, Balsall Heath.

There were two important considerations before that move took place. At the practical level there was the question of feeding the workers attending the factory, and secondly arranging a satisfactory system of payment, within the strictures on allowances.

Initially for their midday meal some walked back to the hospital and some were transported by minibus. Fifty ate lunch at a nearby café but that was the limit for numbers and at a cost of four shillings per head expenditure in greater numbers was too big a drain on finances. By March 1966, after further negotiations, a system was devised where all attenders at the factory received a packed sandwich lunch with hot drinks provided on site, and a full hot dinner was provided by the hospital in the evenings in place of a cooked lunch. In some ways it mirrored changes in society where people were beginning to change from a cooked midday meal to snack meals at lunchtime and a main meal in the evenings. To change this in a rigid hospital setting was quite revolutionary.

The successful launch of a factory in Heaton Street made directors keen to provide a facility that was more easily available to the other Birmingham mental hospitals. The superintendents of the hospitals and the superintendent of the Regional Board's selective rehabilitation unit at St. Wulstans in Malvern were invited on to the Council of the Association, although not involved in the day to day running. The latter was in the hands of an executive committee of eight directors who met regularly.

This proposed move took on an urgency when the Association met its first disaster. On 6th September 1966 the Heaton Street factory was destroyed by fire. Fortunately there were no casualties and a cause was never discovered. Work had to return to the All Saints site while Alderman Thomas with his knowledge of local works negotiated the lease from Birmingham Corporation of the much larger empty factory in Vincent Parade. It had a capacity for 300 against the 75 that could be accommodated in Heaton Street. Vincent Parade was in the middle of a planned redevelopment area which now forms part of the Middle Ring Road in the Balsall Heath/Moseley area. When we moved the duration of our occupation was an unknown factor, but it was at least several years and now it was equally accessible to the hospitals of Rubery, Hollymoor and John Conolly in South Birmingham.

The Lord Mayor of Birmingham formally visited the factory in Vincent Parade on 14th July 1967 by which time it was up and running. The factory had been equipped and repaired under the supervision of Denis Thomas, but much of that work was undertaken by patients as part of their training for a return to outside industry.

At the same time as Vincent Parade was coming into being, negotiations were taking place with the Ministry of Labour to set up a special Rehabilitation Unit within the Vincent Parade factory. From our point of view a method of increasing payment as an incentive for those fit to return to work was essential. It was apparent that money for work done was no less an incentive to the recovering psychiatric population than it was to the general population. We had to work with a rigid ceiling of payment, which if exceeded resulted in benefit cuts, a problem which is no less today than it was in 1966.

Within the limits forced upon us I had devised the basis for an incentive payment system but, once the ceiling was reached within the system, we had to look at other ways of motivating our best workers and the link up with the Ministry of Labour provided that, while it was in existence. For the record the original payment scheme which formed the basis of our payments for many years is reproduced.

SYSTEM OF PAYMENT TO PATIENTS WORKING FOR B.I.T.A.

A system of payments to patients undergoing rehabilitation should contain two essential features:

1. It should reflect the ability and conscientiousness of the individual recipient.

2. It should serve as an index of progress.

The system to be instituted will be based on the following indices:
a) The degree of skill required by the work on which the patient is employed.
b) The conscientiousness which the patient applies to allocated work together with observed output.
c) Attendance.   *contin...*

The implementation of a purely peace-work method of payment is too complicated to apply at present. A payment will therefore be based on a maximum attainable 6/- per day for 5 days per week. The 6/- will be divided into 3/- per day based on (a) and 3/- per day based on (b). (a) will be allocated on a three point scale of increasing skill, each point being the equivalent of 1/-. (b) will be allocated on a 6 point scale, each point being the equivalent of 6d.

Payments will only be made on days of attendance, so that weekly calculations will be made on the formula:

a + b x c = total payment

Thus the minimum a patient working a full week can earn is 7/ 6d.
(1/ - + 6d x 5)   and the maximum initial payment 30/ -

To provide continued financial incentive up to the maximum allowable payment of £1.19.11. A bonus system will operate as follows:

Any patient who has been on the initial maximum of 30/ - for four consecutive weeks will earn a bonus of 2/ - and will continue to receive additional 2/ - bonuses at the end of succeeding four-week periods of maximum pay. Thus by the end of five months a patient who has uninterrupted attendance on maximum pay will be receiving 38/ - and if such a patient completes the full six months will qualify for the maximum allowable 39/ 11d. The upper limit of the bonus payments are almost certainly theoretical as any patient showing this degree of application to a more skilled job over a sustained period will, except in unusual circumstances, be ready to return to normal employment.

A register will be kept of weekly individual payments and can be referred to as one index of progress. Patients should be made aware of the basis on which payment is made and, when receiving their weekly payment, shown how their total has been reached so that they may know how they can increase their earnings.

It is estimated that between thirty and forty patients will be transferred to B.I.T.A. for payment on the 1st June 1966, and that their average earnings to start with will be between 15/ - and 20/ - per week.

Mr. Picton's links with Ministry of Labour civil servants was to lead to the venture with the Ministry of Labour. We had in our favour a period when employment in local industry was readily available. In addition many of the best workers from the long-stay hospital populations in the city were still with us.

The move to Vincent Parade opened the way for other hospitals in the city to participate and before long patients from Rubery, Hollymoor and John Conolly hospitals in South Birmingham were arriving in increasing numbers. Only Highcroft Hospital did not participate in any numbers, preferring to continue to place most patients within their own internal workshop.

The talks with the Ministry of Labour extended over several months but culminated in the establishment of a Ministry backed Rehabilitation Unit within the Vincent Parade factory. A full-time Disablement Resettlement Officer was allocated to the unit and seventy of the best workers from all the participating hospitals attended daily. In addition, another 130 patients in various stages of recovery were attending the other workshops, but in the first six months at Vincent Parade 53 people were placed in open employment.

Although the Lord Mayor of Birmingham formally visited the factory on 14th July 1967, the culmination of recognition came when the Rt. Hon. Roy Hattersley, the Parliamentary Secretary to the Ministry of Labour officially opened the premises on 29th September 1967. It was his first official engagement since taking up his government post.

In many respects this started the summit of the Association's achievements for many years, although it did retain that level for a number of years before economic changes brought the more difficult times that all organisations meet sooner or later. We had succeeded in achieving two important and interdependent objectives: the efficient discharge of our industrial responsibilities, and the rehabilitation of former patients into full time employment.

By the end of 1967 the number attending was still expanding and was 243 by the end of October. This was placing a considerable strain on supervisory staff and without adequate supervision the production potential necessary to keep the enterprise solvent was difficult to attain. We were attracting plenty of orders from sub-contracting firms and had reached the fortunate position of being able to choose the best type of work and the more remunerative jobs. We did secure a very big sub-contract from G.K.N., which was the backbone of a substantial proportion of our work for some years, but in the end was to provoke a crisis that took some time to resolve.

The numbers attending had grown, not only from the South Birmingham hospitals but from further afield. At the end of 1967, there were eleven patients attending from Barnsley Hall Hospital in Bromsgrove, and the provision of hostel places in the city by Birmingham Association for Mental Health under the chairmanship of Mr. Kirk, allowed hospitals from further afield, such as St. Edwards in Leek, Staffordshire to place patients in hostels so that they could attend B.I.T.A. for rehabilitation. The creation of a rehabilitation hospital at St. Wulstans in Malvern by the Regional Board had been aimed specifically at taking such patients from the region's hospitals to St. Wulstans for industrial therapy. However by 1967 most of the hospitals who had initially sent their patients to St. Wulstans were finding that there was less and less movement in and out of St. Wulstans, so that other ways had to be sought to meet the requirements of the growing numbers who were ready to leave hospital through the advances on psychiatric drug therapy, but needing extensive rehabilitation due to the length of time they had been confined in hospitals.

Some hospitals in the region were more aware of the needs for rehabilitation than others and were in the forefront of rehabilitation schemes but by the late sixties all hospitals were aware of the needs and were under pressure to decrease their overcrowded hospitals. Many had few facilities available in terms of community accommodation and advanced retraining programmes. By 1967, B.I.T.A. together with its Ministry of Labour unit was providing the major resource in the region for rehabilitation back to outside employment.

Chapter Four

WEST BROMWICH

At this point it is necessary to digress to deal with another development which had its origins in 1967. This was the setting up of a subsidiary unit in West Bromwich.

At the time the various townships which now constitute the Borough of Sandwell were allocated to various hospitals in the region. Patients in Smethwick went to Highcroft, Tipton to St George's in Stafford, others in Rowley Regis and Oldbury to Barnsley Hall, Bromsgrove, while West Bromwich and Wednesbury were the responsibility of All Saints Hospital. When the Borough of Sandwell was created, common sense prevailed and the whole borough became part of All Saints' catchment area.

Because of the existing links between West Bromwich and All Saints I, as Medical Director of All Saints maintained a close liaison with Dr. Hugh Bryant, who was the Medical Officer of Health for West Bromwich. Dr. Bryant had taken a keen interest in the development of B.I.T.A., and early in 1967 he raised informally in discussion the possibility of setting up a workshop in West Bromwich. This had become an issue after the move from Heaton Street to Vincent Parade meant that patients discharged to West Bromwich were having a good deal further to travel.

In November representatives of Dr. Bryant's Health Committee met with B.I.T.A. directors to further this proposal. The outcome was a suggestion that a disused factory along similar lines to the development in Birmingham be sought with a view to establishing a subsidiary workshop exclusively for patients from West Bromwich and Wednesbury.

In January two possible sites had been identified by the Borough Surveyor. One was the former premises of Joseph Bates (Printers) Limited in Paradise Street, West Bromwich. It was in the ownership of the Corporation, and available until the development of the new town centre, scheduled for 1972.

In February 1968, with Denis Thomas, we visited this factory. It seemed ideal for industrial rehabilitation, would take up to 100 trainees, and required a lot less work to get it ready than had been the case at Vincent Parade. We strongly recommended it for its proposed use to Dr. Bryant and his committee, provided there was an agreement on a peppercorn rental.

With the support of Dr. Bryant matters proceeded steadily. Work had to be done to make the premises suitable for our purposes, the major item putting the heating system in order.

As virtually all of the initial attenders were the responsibility of All Saints Hospital one of the hospital charge nurses, Mr. Thomas Bolter was put in charge, with responsibility to the general manager in Birmingham. Although it was generally recognised that the role of the nurse and factory supervisor were not always compatible due to the conflict in their roles, Mr. Bolter was a nurse who had already a great deal of experience in industrial rehabilitation and was in fact the nurse in charge when the initial car wash was started in Northbrook Street. He remained with the West Bromwich subsidiary throughout its existence and was one of the pillars of the early days of work rehabilitation.

The board of B.I.T.A. decided that it was necessary to set up a separate subsidiary company and the West Bromwich Industrial Therapy Association Limited, or W.B.I.T.A. for short, was formed. Its directors were the same as those on the executive of B.I.T.A. with the addition of Dr. M.A. Shields who was the Deputy Medical Officer of Health for West Bromwich at the time of formation.

The factory in West Bromwich opened on 24th March 1969. The official opening was performed by the Mayor of West Bromwich, Alderman E. Knight on 21st July 1969. By the end of that year 60 patients attended daily. The majority were day patients from All Saints with home addresses in West Bromwich. Referrals were also taken directly from the psychiatric out-patient department at Hallam Hospital and from the West Bromwich Mental Welfare Department. In its first year 28 attenders were placed in open employment and by the end of December 1969 the work in the factory produced an overall profit of £960.

During 1970, 144 people were referred, 103 from All Saints and 41 from local authority and D.E.P. sources. During that year 37 people were placed in open employment, 6 were transferred to the Industrial Rehabilitation Unit in Handsworth, and 8 resumed their roles as full time housewives.

This success rate was particularly satisfactory as W.B.I.T.A. had a high proportion of workers requiring long-term sheltered employment and were not considered suitable for the Ministry of Labour Unit in Vincent Parade. Much of this was due to the enthusiasm of staff allocated to the unit and the resourcefulness of Mr. Bolter. Quite apart from the work, the staff developed a range of social activities in association with workers and relatives and ran evening bus trips, visits to the theatre, and other social events.

The factory in Paradise Street continued to operate with continued success both in a rehabilitative and social sense until 1976 when the redevelopments within West Bromwich made it necessary to relocate. In fact protracted negotiations for a new site began in 1975 and finding premises on an acceptable site proved much more difficult than the initial workshop set up in the former Bates Printing Works. Our time there was one of constant satisfaction with the work that was done, the rehabilitation that was achieved, and the social life that was developed through the efforts of dedicated staff.

The further development in West Bromwich, or Sandwell as it had become will be referred to later in this history.

The workshop in Vincent Parade in the 1960's.

The workshop in Vincent Parade in the 1960's.

The workshop in Vincent Parade in the 1960's.

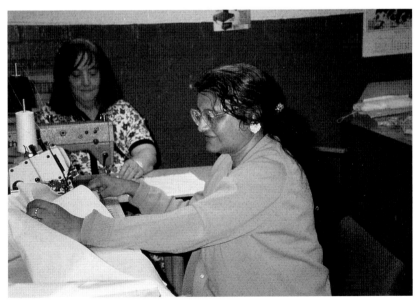

St Anne's Textiles workshop in Saltley. Trainee worker Rattan Soni using one of the industrial sewing machines shortly after the opening of the centre in 1999.

The exterior of the Digbeth premises taken at the time of purchase in 1973 and included in the exhibition in the USA.

The empty workshop in Digbeth taken at the time of purchase in 1973 and included in the exhibition in the USA.

A Christmas social at the Digbeth workshop sometime in the 1980's.

The Digbeth workshop just after opening in 1973.

The final match of a snooker tournament held in the Digbeth work-
shop in the 1980's, presided over by umpire and General Manager
David Underhill in full dress uniform.

Presentation of trophies by General Manager David Underhill.

*General Manager David Underhill with an unknown Father Christmas
at a Christmas social in the Digbeth workshop in the 1980's.*

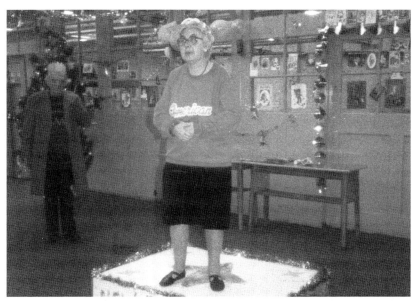

A Christmas social in the 1980's, pre-karaoke days.

A Christmas disco, one of many held at the St Anne's Church Centre in Alcester Street in the mid-1990's.

The exterior of the Digbeth premises after the first refurbishment using funds granted by Economic Development in 1992.

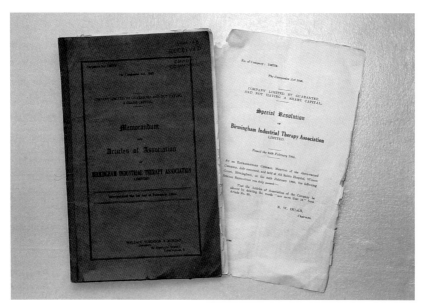

The original Memorandum and Articles promulgated in February 1963.

*A plaque commemorating work undertaken after
a flood in the 1970's at the Digbeth premises.*

Chapter Five

EARLY DAYS: VINCENT PARADE

To return to the activities of the Association in Birmingham, early in 1968 we experienced our first major change in management. It had always been anticipated that Denis Thomas would be with us for a limited time. In April 1968 he resigned after becoming a director of Barmatic. His departure left a sudden predicament. There was still no agreed criteria on what constituted the right background and training for a manager of an industrial therapy organisation to rehabilitate psychiatric patients. Although many used nursing staff because they were an available resource, the majority of nurses did not have the necessary background in industry to negotiate sub-contracted work, establish working procedures for maximum efficiency in production, set up quality controls, and ensure that the workers were achieving a rate of production that would make them acceptable in outside industry. To some extent Mr. Thomas, with advice from directors such as Mr. Kirk did achieve this, but Mr. Thomas' main value had been his political links and his contacts in industry and local government.

These were important in our early days and took a lot of his time. It was apparent however with the rise in numbers attending, the range of work being offered and the higher production requirements of the Ministry of Labour section that we needed somebody who would make us function as close to the requirements of outside industry as it was possible to get, given the wide range of abilities and the differing limitations of our workers.

As managing director, but with major problems to solve and deal with in my statutory role as Medical Director of a large psychiatric hospital undergoing change, I was suddenly faced with an urgent decision, and had an enormous stroke of good fortune. I decided we must have somebody from industry and went to the labour exchange with my problem. It was, by chance, a fortunate time. A number of workers from Dunlop had just been made redundant after completion of a project associated with Concorde. In charge of the section had been Mr. T.H. Williams and he had signed on that week. Mr. Williams was of an age when many men might have contemplated retirement after redundancy. When I met him it was apparent that he was still very fit and active. He was the only suitable person available, but he had no experience of working with people with psychiatric problems. I decided to take a chance and offered him the post of manager, and he took a chance and accepted.

I suspect with his background and experience he would have looked elsewhere if he were younger, but he was realistic enough to know he was of an age when prospects were limited.

It was interesting that right from the outset Mr. Williams ignored the fact that his workers had psychiatric problems. He treated them exactly as he would a normal work force. It was a valuable lesson as he provoked the same response as he would from any other group of workers. They did not become a hundred percent efficient workers overnight and many never did but they responded to the limit of their individual capabilities. His approach was not without problems. Some of the more senior nursing staff, used to a more protective approach to their patients, complained that the manager was driving too hard and causing unnecessary stress. However one of the main lessons we were learning was that psychiatric patients did not differ in their motivations, incentives and responses from the non-psychiatric. We quickly discovered that the most effective single incentive to our workers was money just as it was for other workers, and even within the limits of the amounts we were allowed to pay, this was still the greatest incentive. I now discovered that the methods of success Mr. Williams employed with his section of workers in Dunlop was no less effective with our own workers.

There was however another bonus with the introduction of Mr. Williams. He reorganised our production lines, introduced effective quality controls, and obtained better and more realistic prices from firms for their sub-contracted work. He reviewed our permanent staff and made some overdue changes.

Our continuing existence, then and now, depended on keeping ourselves financially solvent. Although we had plenty of moral support from the statutory services we were aware that such support would dwindle if we became dependent upon them financially for our continued existence. Mr. Williams had to begin by making us more economically viable, and as a result our expenditure was reduced by around £125 per week.

We were fortunate in those early years to have the financial wisdom of Mr. B.T. Davis, a Chartered Accountant, and one of our founding directors. Mr. Davis had all the caution and experience of many years of running his own accountancy firm, and there was no way that he would allow us to become financially dependent. He told us what we had to do and Mr. Williams delivered.

During 1968 we had approximately 250 people attending regularly with 75 in the Ministry of Labour section. The D.R.O. had full responsibility for the selection of those entering the Ministry workshop, and for their placement in outside industry. In 1968 a second full time D.R.O. was allocated to the unit. In the first sixteen months after the opening of the Ministry workshop 170 were placed in full time employment.

Our work in rehabilitation was beginning to have its effect on the hospital, although the Association's role was complemented by the setting up of halfway hostels, lodging schemes and day care. By the end of 1967 the average bed capacity at All Saints Hospital had dropped by 140 from the average bed occupancy at the beginning of 1964 when the Association began to operate. Another statistic at the time showed that by the end of 1967 there were 278 fewer patients with a stay in hospital exceeding five years, compared with 1961.

The road back to independent living of so many after years in hospital had to be gradual and carefully planned. In those early years of running down the overcrowded mental hospitals that gradual approach required the development of support services. It continued this way with many hospitals until the 1980's when the hasty and often poorly planned policies for accelerated closure of the running down hospitals resulted in a stampede of discharges that alienated the community and left many of the more chronic cases in distressed circumstances.

In the 1960s, to ease patients back into the community, day hospitals began to grow. By the end of 1968, places in the day hospitals at, or attached to, All Saints had increased in numbers to 400, one of the three largest in the country. Of those 400, 40% of the men and 20% of the women were undergoing active rehabilitation within the Association, at Vincent Parade, Northbrook Street as well as Paradise Street in West Bromwich.

A survey of the types of work undertaken in Vincent Parade was made at the end of 1968. It not only reflects what work was available to us in the late sixties, it also reflects what types of lower paid jobs were being done in Birmingham at that time;

- Assembling and packaging GKN Pozi-Drive Kits.
- Gauging, inspecting and sorting of screws, nails and rivets.
- Finishing and defazing nuts and bolts.
- Counting and packing car numbers and letters in scores.
- Drilling and tapping plastic parts.
- Deploughing plastic cogs.
- Finishing plugs and sockets.
- Painting and polishing gas cooker knobs.
- Making shopping bags, steering wheel muffs and cushions.
- General repair work, e.g. overalls.
- Making metal letter racks.
- Assembling washers and nuts on spindles.
- Weighing and packing builders copper clips.
- Closing, waiving and raising blanks, various clips for hand presses and the automatic press.

- Carding pencils of various types.
- Tapping and drilling steel bolts.
- Cutting chains into assorted lengths and inserting into Biro pens.
- Fitting rubber plates to invalid chair foot pedals.
- Assembling aircraft parts.
- Assembling electrical terminals.
- Assembling and making miniature wooden Welsh Dressers.
- Assembling central heating radiators.
- Assembling time switches and main switch boxes.
- Assembling various porcelain electrical connectors.

This list shows a wide variety of different skills levels. With the wisdom of the hindsight with which later generations criticise the attempts of previous generations some of those jobs have been castigated as boring or even anti-therapeutic. They overlook a number of reasons why certain things which do not seem right now were relevant in that time and context. First any industrial rehabilitation unit has to reflect the type of work that will be offered in that particular community to rehabilitees when they seek outside employment. If we had been located deep in some rural area, no doubt we would have kept sheep and pigs and grown vegetables. In Birmingham at that time many of the jobs available were simple sorting and assembling of nuts and bolts and screws in many factories. Computers had not arrived and when one sees many of our current trainees sitting hour after hour in front of their computers, one cannot help wondering if some future generation will not condemn that in its turn.

There was another good reason for the various skill levels. It had already become apparent that a proportion of our workers were never going to achieve the level of skill or speed necessary to obtain outside employment. Nevertheless they enjoyed and obtained benefit from coming to work daily with us, and performing at their own level. To turn them away would have returned them to the idleness and isolation that had characterised so much of their lives previously. Starting new referrals on low skills jobs gave an initial indication of potential and those who could not meet the requirements of low level work were unlikely to be able to return to outside employment. Those who did could quickly be transferred to more demanding jobs.

One further development is reflected in the list of types of work. Most of it was sub-contracted, but we were conscious of the need to try and generate our own products so that we were not solely dependent on sub-contractors. It is a dilemma that has continued to exercise us in the Association, and we are still seeking a satisfactory solution. In 1968 we listed the making of shopping bags, wheel muffs and cushions. This came about when somebody suggested we ask the car manufacturers for their upholstery off-cuts. These were given to us in large amounts for a time and we obtained a number of industrial sewing machines and turned them into products such as the shopping bags. They were sold in Payne's Shoe Repair Shop, which at that time had branches throughout the city. Harry Payne, their founder, was a strong supporter of our efforts and his trust made a generous donation in our early days.

Sadly, the off-cuts eventually disappeared, overtaken by progress, and that initial attempt to market our own products dwindled away for some time.

Before leaving 1968, it has to be recorded that our Association's work was beginning to reach a wider audience. At a conference on rehabilitation in Birmingham, I was invited to read a paper on the "Organisation and Development of the Birmingham Industrial Therapy Association". This paper was later published in The British Journal of Social Psychiatry (Vol 2, No 3. 1968). At the end of the paper, I gave a number of reasons to justify our policy towards rehabilitation which are reproduced here as the sum of our whole philosophy.

1. An efficient independent industrial therapy organisation run on a proper commercial basis ensures that the profit arising from the efforts of the patients are wholly and exclusively used for the furtherance of the psychiatric rehabilitation programme, and that such a programme is neither dependent on leftovers after the bulk of NHS money has been allocated, or makes undue claims for money when it can be shown that the work can be self-supporting.
2 It takes the patients on the first essential step back into the community and into conditions similar to that which they will eventually have to face, also the hospital nurse into the community alongside his or her patients.
3. It provides a gradual rehabilitation back to full community responsibility and self-sufficiency, and avoids the sudden changes many patients are unable to make easily or successfully from sheltered conditions inside hospital to outside competitive industry.
4. It provides the non-rehabilitable long-stay patient with interests outside the hospital which helps to counteract the inevitable consequences of having spent many years in an institution.
5. Patients treated this way become better behaved, more alert, and begin to orientate themselves positively towards the outside environment.
6. Finally, it provides an arena for the joint co-operation of all, whether statutory or voluntary, who have to be involved to provide the maximum beneficial results for the returning psychiatric patient.

In that same year there was published a very authoritative and comprehensive King's Fund Report on "Industrial Therapy in Psychiatric Hospitals". We had contributed extensive data to the investigation that preceded that report, and its findings incorporated the data from our Association.

The writer of the report summarised succinctly: "The report of a fact finding survey of industrial units in psychiatric hospitals in England and Wales which establishes the scope of such units and the variations in their management". The publication was followed by a leading article on "Industrial Therapy in Mental Hospitals" in the British Medical Journal of 25th January 1969.

To launch its report the King Edward's Hospital Fund for London held a conference on 25th September 1968 entitled; "The Psychiatric Patient and Sheltered Employment". Among the sessions was the following;

Varieties of Provision in England: Speakers and representatives from:-

i.   Thermega Ltd. – Major J.R. Donnelly
ii. Bristol Industrial Therapy Organisation – Dr. Donal Early
iii. Cheadle Royal (Industries) Ltd – Dr. M.B. Edwards
iv. Birmingham Industrial Therapy Association – Dr. Norman Imlah
v.   Unified Industrial Work Service (The Croydon Concept) – Mr. K. G. Morley

So there we were, BIRMINGHAM alongside those pioneers from BRISTOL, CROYDON and CHEADLE ROYAL, in the forefront of work rehabilitation and at that time, each of us with overlaps in our approach, but each having our own unique contributions.

It was evident that we were now regarded with those who were in the forefront of this type of venture. We had not been the first, and our creation borrowed from the experience and ideas of those who had been the first, such as Bristol. However we had developed, from these, ideas of our own that were at the time unique to us, and in doing so we began to attract a growing number of visitors from other parts of the country and from overseas. We also attracted a number of post-graduate students and professional workers who studied our methods and results and produced papers as a result of those studies.

Chapter Six

VINCENT PARADE TO ALCESTER STREET

Among the earlier studies of our client group was one by Dr. Martin Davies, begun in 1967 and completed in 1969. Dr. Davies had been appointed Consultant at All Saints Hospital and later became a director of the Association. He carried out a prospective study of all patients first attending B.I.T.A. during the last sixteen weeks of 1967. His follow up of this sample showed that 33% were placed in open employment and 22.5% were in the same employment six months later. His figures compared favourably with an earlier report from Bristol where 23% were placed in employment in their first two years. More significantly, it was extremely favourable when compared with figures from hospital-based units. The latter figure was estimated at 10% by Dr. Kidd in Leicester. The results in the Dr. Davies survey looked even more gratifying when, at the time of the survey, the national unemployment figures were around half a million.

There was another important finding that came out of the survey: Dr. Davies showed that people who attended the unit for twelve months without placement in open employment are unlikely to achieve open employment by longer attendance. He emphasised the need for more sheltered workshops for those who were not going to achieve full employment and gradually the organisation within the Association had to recognise that those who did not reach the full employment criteria were becoming the majority of attenders, and that sheltered workshop provision had to exist alongside full-scale rehabilitation.

The survey demonstrated another trend: Industrial Therapy was established with the expectation that the main beneficiaries would be the schizophrenic patients who took up almost three-quarters of mental hospital long-stay places. However an increasing number of people with chronic neurotic illnesses were using our facilities and returning to employment after lengthy absences due to their neuroses.

There were set backs as well. We had to deal with a fire at Vincent Parade in 1969. Fortunately not of the size that destroyed Heaton Street, but we had to be very conscious of the hazards of old premises, and made full use of guidance from the Factory Inspectorate and the Fire Service, both of which gave us much support. The building and services were soon restored and improved in the process.

Fire potential was always a hazard among long-stay psychiatric patients mainly because heavy smoking was so prevalent. Cigarettes were in fact used as rewards in institutions in the days before the physical dangers of smoking were recognised, and the long-stay patient with few comforts was even more reluctant than the general public to accept restrictions on the habit. Fortunately, after those two fires early in our existence our vigilance and strict compliance with fire regulations has avoided any further occurrences, but getting compliance with no smoking areas has become a long and difficult road. Fortunately nobody was ever harmed in our two fires.

In terms of our therapeutic endeavours a more severe setback was all too apparent by 1969, and that was the rate of relapse among schizophrenic patients. Discharge of large numbers of people with schizophrenia only became possible after the discovery of the anti-psychotic drugs in 1954, notably Chlorpromazine, the first of many anti-psychotics classed as Phenothiazines. All of these drugs were administered by mouth or in short lasting injections for initial acute management. It had become clear that the disease only remitted under continued medication and that failure to maintain medication resulted in relapse, sometimes within a few weeks, but usually a few months after the drug was stopped.

Compliance among discharged schizophrenics became crucial but not easy to ensure and by the late sixties it was evident that 40-45% of patients were failing to maintain medication after a year and 70% after two years resulting in ultimate relapse. This was a national or universal problem which is reflected in some statistics of the time. Psychiatric in-patients in Britain fell from 148,000 in 1954 to 125,000 in 1966. However, between 1949 and 1960, annual admissions doubled from 55,000 to 114,000 and in 1964 out of 36,000 admissions, 25,000 were re-admissions. We had reached a situation known as "the revolving door syndrome". In 1964 patients with schizophrenia occupied 13.5% of all hospital beds and used 10% of the N.H.S. budget.

Where there was close supervision, following discharge, relapse rates could be reduced, but care in the community was still in its infancy and the need to have a large experienced work force in the community, although becoming recognised, barely existed.

With our programme for rehabilitation more advanced than many the relapse rates were particularly disruptive, as we would put somebody with good remission into full-time employment with sympathetic employers only to find them having full-blown relapses due to failure to continue medication once they were away from the sheltered supervised environment. This was wholly understandable. The patient felt better, was back at work, and like any other patient as they reach recovery they forget to take their medication. As patients with schizophrenia do not relapse immediately they stop, and as they usually feel better for stopping because any little side-effects are no longer present, they conclude that they do not need the drug, and doubt the word of their psychiatrist that it is necessary to remain on their drugs. When they start to relapse they become too ill to recognise the need to get back on medication and unless they have an alert relative or carer they are back in hospital with full blown relapse and the whole process of treatment and rehabilitation has to start again. Between 1949 and 1960 the figures for second admissions to hospital doubled.

Progress in the field of psychopharmacology was about to relieve the problem of relapse. The pharmaceutical company E.R. Squibb and Sons were the first to develop changes that produced the so-called long acting depot anti-psychotics. They had produced, in the United States, a drug called Fluphenazine Enanthate which lasted an average two weeks by deep intra-muscular injection. It began to be used in Britain but most psychiatrists found it had too frequent and too severe side effects to give it an advantage over the oral drugs, and so its use was limited. The side effects were predominantly the known effects of the Phenothiazines generally in causing a form of Parkinson's Disease, characterised by muscle spasms, tremors and rigidity. These could be controlled to some extent with the oral drugs but were too frequent and severe with the Enanthate form. Squibb then developed a second long acting drug in their laboratories in the United States, Fluphenazine Decanoate.

Because the American Food and Drug Administration did not, for some reason, give permission for clinical trials in the United States of this second drug, the Company asked its British subsidiary to arrange trials in Britain. As a result their Medical Director, Dr. Daniel with whom I had previously collaborated, asked whether I would be prepared to carry out the first clinical trial of this new preparation. A format was agreed and together with my then Senior Registrar Dr. C.Neal, we carried out a limited investigation of the drug in comparison with the existing Enanthate form. We discovered two main findings; First that on average it lasted for a week longer than Enanthate but secondly, and more importantly, it produced substantially less side effects than the Enanthate.

We presented our findings to the very first symposium to be held on the drug in 1968, later published in the Journal of Social Psychiatry. On the basis of this and the other studies that were going on, Squibb marketed the drug in Britain in 1969 under the name of Modecate. I asked Dr. Daniel who gave it that name, and he said he thought of the word one night in bed before going to sleep after playing around in his head with words such as modification and moderation. His idea for a name stuck and Modecate became the first widely used and acceptable long-acting depot anti-psychotic.

Because I had this prior knowledge of the potential of the new product I had begun to think of ways of maximising that potential, and the answer seemed to be the depot drug maintenance clinic. I discussed this with Dr. Daniel and together we agreed that it was the way forward. At All Saints Hospital the Management

Committee agreed to a small pre-fabricated building in the grounds being designated the Modecate Clinic and one part-time senior nurse being allocated to visit patients in the community to give them their Modecate if they could not come to the clinic. In many respects he was the first appointed community psychiatric nurse. Once the clinic was up and running, Dr. Daniel had a small sales force delegated within Squibb to the promotion of Modecate and with it the concept of Modecate clinics.

Other long-acting depot drugs soon followed, chiefly Flupenthixol Decanoate (Depixol), and different psychiatrists chose their own preferences but Modecate remained the market leader for many years. Its impact had a dramatic effect on schizophrenic patients attending rehabilitation, and their attendance then became linked with drug maintenance through the clinic. Our relapse rate of schizophrenia fell very significantly but generally only dramatically where there was a well run depot maintenance clinic. As a result we were able to put people with schizophrenia into employment with a much greater guarantee of them remaining well.

Administrative reorganisation within the N.H.S. in 1969 contributed to making it a very eventful year. From the outset we had received interest and support from the Birmingham Regional Board, and in particular we had received an endorsement from the Ministry of Health which recognised the importance the Ministry allocated to our role as a voluntary body collaborating with the statutory authority. Hitherto the main statutory authority was the All Saints Hospital Management Committee which due to our historical origins provided close support, partially by placing nursing staff in supervisory roles in both factory and car wash. In 1969 the separate psychiatric hospital managements disappeared and we were amalgamated into much larger hospital groupings, each dominated by one of the large general hospitals. Psychiatric health workers viewed this with apprehension, anticipating that their needs would be subordinated to the demands of general medicine and surgery.

This fear was in many ways justified by subsequent events, in some groups more than others. All Saints was amalgamated into the group dominated by Dudley Road General Hospital and a large geriatric hospital. The group also included a number of scattered specialist hospitals such as Eye, E.N.T. and Skin. As far as B.I.T.A. was concerned we had apprehensions on whether the existing supportive links could be maintained. Fortunately they were as three of our directors found themselves on the new group management committee. Mr. Hal Cohen, a prominent schools dentist had been Chairman of the All Saints Management Committee and became Vice Chairman of the new group. Mr. Cohen had been a strong supporter of B.I.T.A. and became a director of the Association following his appointment to All Saints. In addition, I was appointed to the new management committee. However the crucial link was through Mr. B.T. Davis, one of the B.I.T.A. founders, who happened to be the Chairman of the Finance Committee at Dudley Road Hospital and continued in that position in the new group. His dual role greatly eased the transition and arrangements were not disrupted. Mr. Davis did recognise one anomaly that had arisen. Although all seconded staff were being supplied by All Saints, a considerable number of rehabilitees were coming from other hospitals. The solution was for other hospitals to provide proportional support but this had many administrative difficulties. Instead Mr. Davis negotiated a financial arrangement through the Regional Board where appropriate financial payments were taken from other groups and given to the Dudley Road Group on the understanding that they would second sufficient additional staff to meet the supervisory needs of the other hospitals.

Without seconded supervisors we could not have afforded to progress at the rate we were doing. However the hospitals recognised that without us the cost of providing staff for effective rehabilitation would be much greater. Our problem was that this took care of our day to day running costs but left nothing for capital and developments. For this we were dependent on grants, or on profits from our workshops and car wash. Fortunately under Mr. Williams these profits on our industrial work were coming through. An operating surplus in the factory of £4169 increased to £5366 in 1970. The car wash in Northbrook Street which had shown a steadily increasing surplus since its inception until 1969, showed a decrease in 1970, from receipts of £4780 in 1969 to £3873, the operating surplus reducing to £1882, a fall of £630. We now faced a decision over the future of the car wash. The original lease on Northbrook Street was a short one, and was coming to an end. Housing developments around the site were isolating it from main street traffic, hence the fall in receipts.

We had to decide whether to contact the City of Birmingham Estates Department, although some of our directors thought that the development of commercial mechanical car washes could mean that our hand washing service was already becoming redundant. However its value as a rehabilitative job persuaded us to continue car washing and by 1971 we had negotiated with the Estates Department a lease of land in Bacchus Road, Winson Green. Planning permission was granted but the capital for the project had to be found from our own resources.

Two other research projects, both associated with Aston University were produced in 1970. In April Fiona Broughton obtained a B.Sc. in Behavioural Science with a thesis on Industrial Rehabilitation of the Mentally Ill based on the work of B.I.T.A. It was essentially a follow-up study of former rehabilitees. During the time she worked on this she was attached to the Association as an assistant personnel officer with a grant from the Association of Mental Health. In October, Mr. John O'Shea, a nurse tutor, produced a thesis for the Diploma in Health

Services Administration. This was an evaluation of community services provided by All Saints Hospital and B.I.T.A. Both studies provided very useful information in evaluating our work and planning our future although many of the points brought out were becoming familiar.

A particular point brought out in the Broughton study was the fact that many of our rehabilitees were unskilled or semi-skilled and that most were placed in work in the same category. As at least half of our referrals were people with schizophrenia this raised a point that often received criticism through failure to understand the damage that is caused by schizophrenia. Having the illness over a length of time or having repeated acute attacks destroys the ability to think in the abstract. Most skilled work requires the ability to think abstractly and it is a fundamental prerequisite to passing high academic examinations. Consequently many people who get this illness and have hitherto begun in academic work such as teaching, or have shown academic potential at school, can no longer function at that level after breakdown and their occupational sights have to be changed. This can be very frustrating for parents or other people involved who do not understand this change, and it can be frustrating for the recovering patient who tries to resume studies or return to work requiring abstract thinking. One patient of mine, the brightest in his year in a very academic school, after acute schizophrenia, progressed through increasingly less academic jobs until he found his niche as a member of an industrial cleaning team.

The other result of this disability is that the person with schizophrenia does best at work that is repetitive and therefore boring to the non-schizophrenic. Thus it is the unskilled or semi-skilled job requiring a minimum of abstract thinking where there is the best chance of successful employment.

Although the psychiatric hospitals in North and South Birmingham continued to provide most referrals it was noticeable by 1970 a growing number were coming from non-hospital sources. In 1970, out of a total of 331 referrals, 81 were from non-hospital sources such as general practitioners, mental welfare officers and employment exchanges. In addition, Shelton Hospital in Shrewsbury, Powick Hospital near Worcester and St. Edwards Hospital at Leek in Staffordshire made use of our services, due to the provision of hostel places for their rehabilitees in the city provided by the Birmingham Association for Mental Health. In 1970, there were 35 referrals from these outside hospitals. In total in 1970 I have counted 21 different referral sources. At that time they all came under the responsibility of the seconded nursing staff, and with the introduction of new grading systems within nursing, the nurse with overall responsibility was designated Nursing Officer Grade 7. In 1970 he defined his nursing responsibilities as follows:

1. *Maintenance of daily register of attendance.*
2. *Requisitioning of stores, drugs and meals.*
3. *Payments to patients.*
4. *Re-imbursement of travel expenses.*
5. *Allocation of bonus incentive payments to those not in receipt of hospital allowances.*
6. *Accountability to the Hospital Finance Committee.*
7. *Maintenance of the Factories Act Register.*
8. *Records of patients attending and reports on them to referral sources.*
9. *Responsibility for the selection of patients.*
10. *Act for General Manager in his absence.*

Inevitably there were difficulties with this dual management structure. The No 7 Nursing Officer was responsible directly to his own hierarchy within the hospital, in the first instance to a No 8 who had all of rehabilitation under his wing, and he in turn to the No 9, formerly the Hospital Matron or Chief Male Nurse. The General Manager on the other hand was directly responsible to the directors of the Association through the Managing Director, who had to intervene when they reached an impasse.

The role of the General Manager was well-defined over the years but with inevitable changes in nursing personnel, it was the personality of the nursing officers and their perceptions of their role that made for a more harmonious or less harmonious relationship in areas where their roles overlapped. One of these was in (9) Responsibility for the selection of patients, and the conflicts between seeing a person as benefiting from attendance as seen by the nurse but useless as a worker as seen by the factory manager was but one example of conflicting views.

The point (10) of the Nursing Officer acting for the General Manager, in his absence, was not satisfactory because of these conflicting roles and the perception of other staff within the workshop of two distinct chains of command. In April 1970 this was resolved by the appointment of a Deputy General Manager, which our growth now justified. It was a significant appointment in terms of the future of the Association and worth recording. Mr. Williams recommended Mr. David Underhill who was already working with us as a supervisor on the floor as his deputy and this was agreed by the Board. His wife Olive Underhill had joined the Association in 1965 as secretary/bookkeeper and through that link her husband came to work as a floor supervisor. Both were to remain with the Association until their joint retirement, Olive becoming Company Secretary and David Underhill succeeding Mr. Williams as General Manager.

Another area of disagreement was payment. A letter from the Nursing Officer in January 1971 begins; "I am rather unhappy about the situation between Mr.

Williams and myself. This concerns the payments to patients of pocket money and travelling expenses". The letter then goes on to deal with some individual cases. These disputes arose from time to time and were not always easy to resolve as they both saw this from their different perspectives, but were equally sincere in their viewpoint. Even though the general guidelines were laid down individual anomalies would crop up and sometimes required intervention and an arbitrary judgement on the individual merits.

The start of 1971 saw developments that were much more fundamental to our future. Early in January Mr. Williams and I met with representatives of the Public Works and Housing Departments to discuss the situation arising out of the expiration of our lease of Vincent Parade in March 1974. Even though we had three years to run the area around us in Balsall Heath was earmarked for demolition to make way for the Middle Ring Road and it was clear that most of it would be demolished well before the expiry of the lease, and that we would run into inevitable problems, including vandalism and operating within a desert of demolition.

The obvious solution was to be offered alternative factory premises but that would almost certainly involve another short-term lease and the disruptions of preparing another old building for habitation. More seriously, the City representatives thought it very unlikely that they could offer us another suitable building with a similar central location, although there would not be a difficulty in offering us an alternative away from the centre. Because the Association was now committed to having its main facility readily accessible to all the major psychiatric centres this was a matter that required urgent consideration by the Board.

There was no immediate answer. Although the concept of acquiring permanent premises was favoured, it was evident that we needed to initiate discussions with statutory bodies and explore the means by which finance for such a venture might be secured. Although on paper our lease had some time to run it was evident that the City Estates found our continuing occupation of Vincent Parade inconvenient and were applying pressure to move early. However the only building in the area which they could suggest was the vacated Moseley Fire Station and Mr. Williams and I examined this but found it to be quite unsuitable.

Our problems in finding new premises were, at this juncture, made more difficult by disagreement among the Directors. While Mr. Picton the Chairman, Mr. Davies, Mr. Cohen and myself in the main executive roles were in accord, Mr. Kirk began to express views over proposals that were not in agreement. Mr. Kirk had in fact been one of the main driving forces in the setting up of the Association, his knowledge of industry was invaluable, and his drive and imagination had been crucial to our beginnings. However those same qualities which were invaluable in the beginning made it difficult for him to work within the constraints required to sustain the goodwill and approval of the various statutory bodies with whom we had to keep on board to survive, and whose approval we enjoyed. We also had responsible roles within the statutory health services and we could continue to pioneer a project outside, provided that outside those roles did not clash with our obligations to the statutory authority.

The situation was not helped by the fact that Mr. Kirk's own industrial firm was having problems, and his business relationship outside the Association, with Mr. Davis, which hitherto had been close, ran into problems that led to a severance of their business links. Some of these outside problems spilled over. Mr. Kirk was against the setting up of another car wash. He had suggestions for a factory site, which were not agreed, but most of all he saw the Association like some outside business and proposed that we should be setting up a chain of industrial therapy units throughout the country. This latter was quite unacceptable to his fellow directors who saw themselves as firmly responsible only for Birmingham, the West Bromwich subsidiary being an exception, because that area was responsible to a Birmingham based hospital for its mental health services.

The idea of setting up a chain of industrial units came from the amount of interest that was being taken in the Birmingham scheme. For example; in 1971-72 both Coventry and Wolverhampton set up working parties composed of health and local authority committee members, with managers and doctors to consider setting up similar therapy units. Both Mr. Picton and myself sat with these working parties and gave them our opinions based on our experiences. However, having done that, we then left them to proceed with their own plans. We did agree with Coventry however, at their request, to have Mr. Williams work with them and advise until their industrial workshop was set up and running.

These differences grew to the extent that Mr. Picton suggested to Mr. Kirk that he resign as a director. While I could only agree that this was in the best interests of the Association it was a matter of deep personal regret as he had done much to further the cause of mental health in the city. Like many self-made men in industry he was not easily thwarted and his energy and enterprise were invaluable in our early days.

By September 1972 it was apparent, after many discussions, that a firm decision on the future was required and I sent the following; "Proposals on Future Requirements Within The Birmingham Industrial Therapy Association" to the Chairman for Board consideration and approval. "As we approach the expiration of the lease on our factory premises in Vincent Parade I consider that, on the basis of our experience until now, and our current predicaments, we should adopt two fundamental items of policy over our next factory:

1. It should be a permanent site.
2. It should be somewhere larger than our present factory.

In support of these points I submit the following :

a) Our current numbers are 312 on the register at Vincent Parade and 97 at West Bromwich. I am informed that we could register approximately another 50 people, but our accommodation is full.

b) The steadily increasing numbers of individuals who leave us to enter full-time employment, e.g. 74 in 1969; 105 in 1970; 117 in 1971.

c) The increasing sources of referral. Currently we receive people from 23 different sources. A noticeable feature, contributing to the more recent increase in the demand for our services, has been the expanding request from community based services. There were 134 referrals in 1971 and currently 112 of those attending Vincent Parade are from community based services.

d) The increase in these referrals seems, to me to be related to the wider general application of concepts of community care which I believe our organisation has done a great deal to foster in the Birmingham area. National policies on community care are now being applied, quite suddenly, on a greater scale and many agencies have turned to us to assist them in the practical application of these policies. Whereas, with patients in hospital, some of those hospitals use their own industrial therapy units or hospital based workshops, the agencies in the community, without access to those workshops, are coming to us with their rehabilitation problems.

e) Despite improvements in treatment and the community concepts of care there is, as yet, no diminution in the need to provide a positive rehabilitation programme for people who have experienced a major mental breakdown.

I think we have proved our ability to successfully return people to full-time employment and that our success in this is recognised locally by the increasing demands that are made upon us. With the continuing promotion of community care concepts, and at the same time an undiminished need for ex-patients to undergo a positive rehabilitation programme, I consider that the two items of policy submitted are fully justified on any assessment of the current situation".

I have reproduced this proposal in full for a number of reasons; Mainly it was definitive of the belief that we had some permanent role and that a unit such as ours had established its place in the scheme of things. When we began it was as an experiment and even if successful, possibly on a limited time-scale. We now believed that the experiment was over, was successful, and here to stay.

It also gives some figures which illustrate the extent of our progression after seven years and the speed of that expansion. Finally it is a snapshot of the emergence of care in the community for the mentally ill. By 1970-71 it had emerged as a reality nationally and in Birmingham we were at the forefront of this change. At that stage we did not know how far it was going, nor could we foresee some of the disasters that lay ahead when mistakes were to be made in application of the policy. That it was right at the time we had no doubt, but it was a transition that required careful planning, and in those early days of application we did feel our way with care.

The proposition received immediate approval from the Board, but this was to be expected as I was well aware that the other directors were in favour from our discussions, and the letter was merely setting down what we had already agreed informally. Having finally reached a decision we had now to act.

Mr. Picton and Mr. Davies, using their wide range of contacts in the N.H.S., Local Authority and Department of Employment set about obtaining the agreement and approval of key people in those places in support of our decision, and at the same time exploring the means by which the necessary finance could be gained. Much of the latter fell upon Bernard Davis who as head of his own firm of Chartered Accountants, and as wise and astute a financial advisor as I have ever encountered, was the ideal person. The total capital we required, including provisions for a new car wash unit was £70,000. Allowing for working capital, the Association had £17,000 available from its own resources towards the cost of purchase.

At the same time, with Mr. Williams, I set about the task of finding suitable premises within a central location that fell within our projected costs. We eventually found such premises at 201-206 Alcester Street, Digbeth. It had been empty for twelve months but was in very good condition, infinitely better than the factories we had been used to hitherto. It extended round the corner from Alcester Street to Warwick Street, and while it was mainly freehold, a small area remained leasehold.

We obtained the customary reports upon the property, which were favourable. It was not affected by any existing town planning proposals. The structure was sound and apart from redecoration and general repairs to roofs, windows and gutters, some due to disuse, the costs of making it ready for use were not excessive, although replacement of boilers was desirable. The initial costs of purchase were higher than we wished, but after negotiation a purchase price of £52,500 was agreed. The purchase was completed during January 1973.

The efforts of Mr. Picton and Mr. Davies had procured the necessary finances but most credit must go to the sympathetic reception from the City of Birmingham Social Services Committee and the Birmingham Regional Hospital Board. As a result the Social Services Committee approved a loan of £53,000 to add to our own contribution of some £17,000, and this loan was to be repaid, without interest, over a period of fifteen years. The repayments of the loan were underwritten by the Birmingham Regional Hospital Board, and David Perris the Chairman of that Board, who took a keen interest in the work of the Association, was the influence behind that guarantee.

The loan not only covered the cost of the new premises and its alterations but covered the costs of building a new car wash on the leased land in Bacchus Road. The final cost of the Alcester Street factory, including alterations and repairs was £56,000 of which £39,000 came from the loan and the remainder from our own resources. The balance of the loan, £14,000 was put toward the new car wash, estimated at £21,600. This meant finding the balance for the car wash ourselves resulting in our ultimate contribution to the factory and the car wash totalling £24,600.

On 31st May 1973, repairs, alterations and decorations being completed, we moved from Vincent Parade to 210-206 Alcester Street.

Chapter Seven

FIRST FIVE YEARS IN ALCESTER STREET

Despite the upheaval of relocating, and the diversion of workers in getting our new factory ready we had satisfactory results for 1973. Despite the move sales increased with an operating surplus of £2,159 after having to pay interest on a bridging loan from the bank at the time of purchase. We also had a surplus of £1052 on Northbrook Street and an investment income of £522. These surpluses came after all allowances to workers were paid and we were often asked to justify our surpluses and reasons for not returning them in some form to the workers. The fact was that the only capital at our disposal was our trading surplus, and this capital was essential to improving conditions and expanding our services. Without it we could not have progressed.

Numbers of new referrals during 1973 were 469 of which 147 went to the Department of Employment section. In the course of the year 157 went to open employment, 87 from DEP and 70 from the rest of the workshop.

In other ways 1973 was a year of immense achievements, and in some ways we reached a pinnacle. Not only did we move, with acclaimed support, to our own permanent site, but our efforts in Birmingham reached a much wider audience and particularly in the United States. Personally it was the busiest year of my working life. Quite apart from the work involved in obtaining and moving to our permanent home, the work on long-acting anti-psychotic drugs together with the setting up of the first depot maintenance clinic and the associated community developments was attracting many visitors, and increasing demands to speak at conferences both at home and abroad.

The time spent on requests to present our work abroad reached a peak in 1973 with three visits to the United States, but as the work of B.I.T.A. occupied a prominent part in those presentations they occupy a significant part in its history. These particular visits came about through E.R. Squibb, the pharmaceutical company responsible for the most prominent depot drug at the time, Fluphenazine decanoate (Modecate). They were anxious that our results should be presented in the United States as the particular drug was still not available there, and they suggested that I present an exhibit on Community Care in Birmingham at the annual meeting of the American Psychiatric Association to be held in Honolulu, Hawaii. As somebody said to me there: "You sure are lucky it was this year; Next year we are in Detroit".

It was agreed that the work of B.I.T.A. would be prominently featured in the exhibit, and many pictures were taken including some of the empty factory in Alcester Street before we moved in. Squibb provided a man whose job it was to put exhibits together and with his help we presented "A Planned System of Community Care for Schizophrenia in Great Britain" at the meeting of the American Psychiatric Association in May 1973. In the seven page brochure which was produced to give to visitors to the exhibition, the work of B.I.T.A. occupied nearly two pages.

In that brochure I listed the total care requirements of a schizophrenic patient as follows:

1. An initial period in an acute hospital.
2. An active comprehensive day hospital.
3. A community psychiatric nursing team linked to a special clinic for maintenance of medication.
4. An industrial therapy organisation specially geared to the needs of the psychiatric patient and reflecting the employment opportunities available in the area.
5. Availability of hostels, halfway houses and approved lodgings.
6. Access to a social club, preferably outside the hospital.
7. Periodic review by the doctor responsible for after-care supervision.

The brochure ended with the following conclusion:

"Great progress has been made in the last twenty years in alleviating the distress of the schizophrenic and in diminishing the destructive course of the disease, but we are still some way from a true cure for the condition. Despite the substantial improvements that can be obtained with psychotropic drugs, we consider that the improvement in outlook for patients with schizophrenia can only be obtained by combining such treatment with a vigorous application of all of the approaches we have presented. Schizophrenia remains a dreadful and destructive disease. We hope that, with this programme, we are ensuring that those who are afflicted with this disease have an infinitely better prognosis than in the past. We emphasise, however, that we have still a long way to go before we can feel satisfied".

That was written in 1973. Now thirty years later one could say almost exactly the same with equal relevance.

Our presentation was extremely well received, and culminated in our being given the prestigious Bronze Award of the American Psychiatric Association, the first time I believe the award was made to an exhibit from outside the United States.

Our success led to an invitation to present the exhibit at the annual meeting of the American Medical Association in New York in July 1973. It was a huge event, and the opening ceremony was attended outside by a number of vociferous protest groups, among them women on abortion issues and gay rights groups. It caused the comedian Bob Hope, who made the opening speech, to quip, "Did you notice that all the mounted police are riding side-saddle this morning?"

Our exhibit in the psychiatric section attracted a lot of interest, including the general public, who were much more prominent than in Hawaii. Many were parents anxious to discuss how our programme could help their schizophrenic offspring. However it was evident on talking to them that many had children with learning difficulties whom they chose to believe had schizophrenia, but interesting to observe that having a schizophrenic son or daughter appeared more acceptable than having one who had a learning retardation.

At the end of the week our exhibit was awarded the Certificate of Merit of the American Medical Association as the most prestigious exhibit in the Section of Psychiatry. As a result we were invited to send the exhibit to the annual meeting of American Hospital Administrators at Miami, Florida in September of the same year where our community care programme created great interest among the administrators anxious to reduce the size of their large psychiatric institutions.

Thanks to the excellent efforts of Mr. Williams and his staff these diversions did not hinder the smooth transition of change, and the continued growth in profits from the workshop. However with the projected new car wash we did hit snags which delayed its opening until May 1974. The main stumbling block was the length of lease of Bacchus Road. Officers in the City Estates wanted to cut this to ten years, which in view of the cost of the new car wash was not acceptable. With the help and intervention of friends on the Council this was eventually agreed as a minimum of fifteen and a maximum of twenty five with a guarantee of six months notice after the end of fifteen years. This delayed the work, and the costs increased from the original estimate. This did not help the arguments of those directors who wanted a new car wash against those who considered it a poor commercial proposition.

The latter were to be proved correct commercially as the new car wash never reached the financial success of the original, but the disagreement was the recurring one of commercial viability against the therapeutic benefit. It was the therapeutic benefit which decided this particular issue, and the financial success in the factory work meant that we could now continue an operation that might not contribute any profits. Car washing had many benefits for the former long-stay patients that we were trying to rehabilitate. It gave them the opportunity to meet and interact with the general public, they had to work as a team, and there was a variable level of skills through which there could be progression. It had also a satisfactory end-product which was a source of satisfaction to the team of workers when they were doing a good job.

Having resolved the question of premises in Birmingham, we were already in the process of looking for other premises in West Bromwich. The lease of the factory in Paradise Street was coming to an end with the imminent development of the centre of West Bromwich and by 1974, we were actually engaged in looking for a replacement, and in negotiations with the relevant authorities.

During 1974 our progress, financially and therapeutically, continued. We had an operating surplus in the factory of £10,277 compared with £2159 in 1973, offset by a loss of £160 in the car washes (Northbrook Street till May 1974 and Bacchus Road from May 1974). During 1974 the number of rehabilitees passing through the workshop remained high. Out of 389 returning to the community, 121 were placed in paid employment (31%), 57 relapsed and required re-admission to the referring hospital for further treatment (14%) although there was some considerable variation to the percentages from hospital to hospital.

In the meantime, political changes had produced the Manpower Services Commission and their Employment Services Agency which we trusted would provide the same support that we had enjoyed from the Department of Employment. Early in 1975 we had a visit from Sir Denis Barnes, Chairman of the Manpower Services Commission who was very sympathetic to our aims so that we had every hope that the favourable relationship would continue. However, despite the obvious goodwill, economic and other factors were about to change in ways that were to interrupt the smooth progression.

Perhaps the first indication that changes were in progress came with a letter in November 1975, from the Operations Manager of the Employment Agency saying that the two Disablement Resettlement Officers based in our Ministry of Labour unit were to be transferred to the Edgbaston Employment Rehabilitation Centre. They justified this as a best use of staff resources and a reassurance that Mr. Adkins the DRO from the formation of our unit would give us the same service as before. Mr. Adkins had in fact been an enthusiast from the beginning and the success of the MOL unit owed a great deal to his enthusiasm and efforts.

It was a matter for concern, but not a total surprise. Most of the better workers from the long-stay hospital populations had been rehabilitated, and at the same time jobs were becoming harder to find as illustrated by this quote from an article on rehabilitation from The Birmingham Post of September 25th 1975, which begins: "While unemployment soars and even the young and the qualified cannot find jobs, there is always hope".

When we reviewed 1975 with a view to our annual report these changes were reflected. Our sales for the year had increased and the number of new referrals was maintained, but the numbers discharged to open employment fell to 52. The two main factors in this drop were identified as the rise in unemployment generally, and the poorer potential of referrals. The better prospects from hospital long-stay had been rehabilitated but the type of referral was changing.

For the first time, patients with schizophrenia comprised less than half the total referrals with a corresponding increase in referrals with deep seated personality disorders and related problems. It was evident that where an active organisation had been operating for some time, most of the acceptable cases had already been rehabilitated, and we were dealing now with a hard core of more difficult cases, and even with cases we would not have considered a few years previously.

It was evident that rehabilitation of the psychiatric patient in the future could become more difficult and challenging, and that we would soon have to consider policy changes to meet the new trends. Paradoxically, because we were no longer losing our best workers when they were ready for discharge to open employment, our workshop output and efficiency were increased and our profits reflected this fact. However, in view of the coming needs for new initiatives any increases in profits were a welcome source of funds for perceived changes.

The most worrying of the changes was the inevitable decline in numbers going into the Ministry unit. With it came a growing disinterest from the Manpower Services Commission. As they found it more difficult to place people in a time of high unemployment, they then became less enthusiastic in filling their 75 places with other rehabilitees, citing the lower calibre of client for the reduction.

While this change was taking place we were continuing to search for a replacement factory in West Bromwich. Attempts initiated by ourselves, talks with officials, involvement of local and national politicians, including the local M.P. Betty Boothroyd, to find funding sources, all failed to produce the necessary finances for our desired option which was to replicate our own Alcester Street premises somewhere in West Bromwich. It was apparent that a move to somewhere similar to the Paradise Street premises was our only option provided a suitable site could be found. There was no lack of willingness locally to help but it was probably influenced by the prevailing economic climate at that time.

By early 1977 the situation in West Bromwich had become critical. The Sandwell Community Health Council had become involved in the urgent need for new premises. They, as part of their campaign, brought the West Bromwich Members of Parliament, Betty Boothroyd and Peter Snape, to the Paradise Street premises which were then in their third year of notice to quit without a suitable alternative. The best alternative suggested was an empty factory in Alberta Road, Smethwick which was not an ideal location. The main stumbling block however was the short term lease of five years which was offered and which the Association perceived as too short, even as a temporary expedient, in view of the amount required to make the factory conversions necessary before it could be ready for occupation. The efforts of the Community Health Council and the involvement of the two local M.P.s gave a much needed impetus to Sandwell officials to find the funds necessary to provide an alternative. As the local newspapers pointed out at the time, failure to find an alternative would result in 90 to 100 former patients being without occupation and having nowhere to go during the day. Interviews with ex-patients in Paradise street illustrated their distress at the prospects of closure without an agreed alternative.

On 21st January 1977 we had a letter from the Chief Executive of the Borough of Sandwell offering us the Alberta Works in Oldbury Road, Smethwick with the Area Health Authority agreeing to the necessary finance for adaptation of the premises. As such finance was only available in the current financial year up until the end of March we had to make an urgent decision, and decided immediately to accept the offer.

Despite the urgent need to earmark the finance of eleven and a half thousand pounds for conversion, the actual work took longer than hoped and the transfer from Paradise Street to Alberta Works eventually took place on 5th September 1977 by which time another three and a half thousand pounds was required to finance the work.

Meanwhile in Birmingham, during 1977, relationships with the Area Office of the Manpower Services Commission were deteriorating predominantly due to the decline in the numbers going through their section and the perceived poorer potential of referrals. Some of this was inevitable for the reasons already given, but some were brought about by changes in attitude and application within the local Employment Service Agency. Mr. Adkins who had been the DRO since the MOL sector was set up retired. The success of the scheme owed much to Mr. Adkins who regularly visited hospitals and clinics to recruit suitable rehabilitees. His successor did not see that mobility as part of his role, and former hospital contacts and close liaisons were gradually lost leading to an inevitable decline in hospital referrals, but the fundamental problem remained the poor general employment situation.

Although these facts were the root of the situation, the Agency in order to justify its declining interest raised objections that had always existed, but where hitherto we had agreed to differ. The main one was their view that workers in their section should be physically separated from other workers. They would consistently underline this point by referring to their section as 'rehabilitees' and those outside the section as 'patients'. We could not accept this distinction as there was a graduation from one to the other and much overlap. Many of the workers not selected by the Agency were better workers than those selected but were less attractive to the Agency in appearance and habit. To emphasise the separation the Agency wanted their work to be totally separate from the work of the rest of the factory. In view of the overlap in skills between those selected and those rejected our Works Manager found it very difficult to maintain a solid commercial work flow if his best workers were artificially separated. Other differences arose over the level of payments to the Agency section workers. These enhanced payments were borne partly by the E.S.A. and partly by B.I.T.A. and over time the proportions began to vary despite a firm initial agreement.

It was clear that the time had come for a thorough re-evaluation of our role and policy. Over the years the policy of the Association had been determined by an executive committee of six - seven directors who met regularly with the managing director and the works manager. Over the years other interested and involved people were invited to become members of the Council. They were kept regularly informed but were not expected to get involved in the running of the Association apart from any input they might care to have at an A.G.M. Among Council members was the Chairman of the Regional Health Authority, Sir David Perris, The Chairman of the Birmingham Area Health Authority, Mr. John Bettinson and the Chairman of Birmingham Social Services, Councillor Frank Carter. All three maintained a very supportive interest in the Association and were readily available for advice and help when required. Councillor Carter did in fact become a member of the executive committee for a number of years. After discussion with the Chairman, Mr. Picton, it seemed time to call a special meeting of the full Council to review our position and produce a policy for the future. A full Council met on 12th January 1978 and as a consequence the Chairman and myself drew up a 'Policy Agreed By Council' which was ratified by the Council and became our blueprint for the future. In the document we outlined the past history and origins, and then dealt with the changes in the type of referral, in many cases more challenging than those of ten years previously. In addition we acknowledged that over the years we had accumulated a considerable body of referrals who were not going to make outside employment, but nevertheless obtained support and gratification from their sheltered employment.

The Council acknowledged the unsatisfactory employment position and the decline in the employability potential of referrals. We had always had a very open policy of accepting anybody who was well enough and not positively disruptive, but we were now finding that some referrals were being sent to us as a 'last resort' and not as being potential rehabilitees. Worse, in some cases the referral source considered that their referral to B.I.T.A. absolved them from any further responsibility or involvement. It was evident that amongst the referral sources there was a very uneven awareness of our proper purpose. It was evident that the system of referral and liaison over cases was no longer adequate. In the beginning referrals had been through an All Saints Hospital Nursing Officer based at the factory. This system worked adequately during the formative years when there were many referrals of a very similar type. It was now evident that a more formal contact, with better selection and a two way communication involving a better defined responsibility between the referring agency and ourselves, had to be implemented.

The Council recognised that there was still a great many people who could benefit. There was still an abundant supply of work of the type, which the Association had specialised in, and provided there were sufficient referrals of reasonable quality the Association could continue to generate funds, which could be ploughed into rehabilitation. It was evident that B.I.T.A. continued to enjoy the support of the local health authorities and the Birmingham local authority.

The Council then made a number of recommendations. The first was the appointment of a full time administrative assistant to create and manage a formal referral and monitoring system, maintain a liaison system with the sources of referral, and establish collaboration with the Employment Services Agency. Along with the latter was a resolve to seek discussions with officers of the E.S.A. to clarify policy objectives.

It was agreed to ask the Regional Health Authority personnel officer, to advise in the management structure within B.I.T.A. There was also a resolve to strengthen the Committee by recruiting new and interested directors particularly those with a medical, nursing and social work background.

The policy document concluded "It is clear that developments in health and community services in relation to rehabilitation have changed the nature of the contribution that pioneers like B.I.T.A. are now required to make. The re-definition of respective responsibilities is an urgent necessity, and it is hoped that this expression of the current policy envisaged by B.I.T.A. would prove to be both a useful initiation of consultations with the aforementioned authorities and also a means of strengthening the framework of collaboration".

Getting a policy document is one thing, but getting it implemented is another. In the end all the main recommendations were put in place after consultation , but it all took time, and despite them there was little improvement in relationships with the E.S.A.

The acceptance of a new policy directive was to be Mr. Picton's last last major contribution to B.I.T.A. In November 1978 he informed me of his intention to retire on the grounds of ill-health. This came rather suddenly and we were ill-prepared. He was a man of great integrity who had the respect of all the authorities with whom we had to deal. His standing within government and local bodies was such that in our formative years and throughout his near fifteen years in the Chair the respect and regard in which he was held was automatically conveyed to the Association by virtue of his position with us. He was generally a wise counsellor and a moderating influence on some of the wilder suggestions of his fellow directors. I found him to be unfailingly supportive, not an initiator of policy, but always ready to make overtures on our behalf when he had been convinced of the direction we should take. I hoped that he might continue to make a contribution but although I saw him from time to time after his retirement it was evident that his health was indifferent and after the death of his wife he tended to withdraw from public affairs, although not entirely without interest in our developments.

His retirement caused an unforeseen dilemma, as none of the other executive directors were inclined, for various reasons, to assume the role of Chairman. As Glyn Picton had been our establishment figure I consulted with Sir David Perris and John Bettinson. There was no obvious immediate replacement from within the statutory authorities. Until such could be found it was agreed that I should assume the role of Chairman until a suitable successor was found. Many years later all those who were in authority then have left the scene, and with no alternative suggestion ever forthcoming I was eventually confirmed in the role of Chairman.

Chapter Eight

ADAPTING TO ADMINISTRATIVE CHANGES

It seems appropriate to begin a new chapter in our history with a revised policy and a new chairman. In February 1979, Dr Martin Davies resigned on his appointment to a new post at the University. He had carried out some valuable research during his time as a Director, and it was always helpful to have a consultant psychiatric colleague, but his resignation accentuated the need for new directors. We complemented this by making three important additions to our executive directors, to improve the range of professional advice available. Dr. Alan Ogden, a Consultant Psychiatrist at Rubery Hospital had been a firm supporter of B.I.T.A. from the beginning of the involvement of the hospitals from South Birmingham. Dr. Ogden is still on the Board and one of our senior directors. Another appointment from the hospitals in the south was Dr. Raychoudri, the Consultant responsible for rehabilitation at Hollymoor Hospital. We were sorry to hear of Dr. Raychoudri's death when in retirement earlier this year. The third appointment was our first nurse on the Board, Mr. M. O'Leary who had risen to be Senior Nurse at All Saints Hospital and had a great deal of experience of B.I.T.A. through his management of seconded nursing staff. Mr. O'Leary remained on the Board until recently when he returned to Ireland following his retirement.

The other matter, which had been long delayed was the appointment of the administrative assistant, but in early 1980 Janice Ledbrook was appointed to the position with a fairly wide brief.

However a good deal of administrative time was taken up by negotiations over our continued presence in Sandwell. We recognised after the move to the former Alberta Works that we were now providing simply a sheltered workshop for ex-patients living in Sandwell. The premises had faults and the location was not ideal for access. Our biggest problem area however was the attempt by Sandwell Local Authority to charge for rent and rates which we considered to be unreasonable particularly as the parent Association was now having to subsidise the West Bromwich factory to some extent. Our point was that we were a charity providing a service to the community, and hitherto authorities had taken an understanding view in leasing us disused premises. Although we were in receipt of agreed joint funding grants there remained a financial gap that we were not prepared to meet indefinitely if it was to be to the detriment of our main function.

To some extent the matter was brought to a head by the first visit of the recently formed Hospital Advisory Service to All Saints Hospital and its catchment area which included all of the Borough of Sandwell. The H.A.S. was not entirely a popular innovation in its early days in the areas where it descended. It tended on the basis of a short visit from three members to issue a report containing a catalogue of critical comments together with a set of dictatorial remedies, which owed as much to the philosophy of the H.A.S. members as they did to realistic solutions to difficult local problems. However as they did so with complete government backing, local administrators felt compelled to meet any recommendations within any H.A.S. report. In their visit late in 1979 they recommended the closure of the Alberta Works Factory and the responsibility of the care of the people attending to be transferred to the Sandwell Social Services.

Although we had some doubts about whether the future of a workshop run by a charity really came within the remit of the H.A.S. it gave us the lever to negotiate with the Sandwell Health and Social Services. In view of the problems since the closure of Paradise Street we considered it better for us to close our West Bromwich subsidiary provided we could be assured of the future of the 90 ex-patients who were in the workshop. The authorities in Sandwell were equally anxious to respond to the H.A.S criticism that the local authorities were not providing facilities themselves for chronically disabled psychiatric cases within the Borough.

Eventually a crucial meeting took place between our directors, and representatives from Sandwell Area Health Authority and Sandwell Social Services Department on 30th April 1980. At that meeting we expressed the view that our workshop should continue to function, but the time had come for it to be run by the statutory authority as a joint A.H.A and S.S.D responsibility in line with the H.A.S. recommendation. However we had to point out that if the statutory authorities did not take over the workshop it was likely that we would eventually have to close it down. At their request we gave a guarantee to run the workshop until the end of March 1981 while they considered their position.

At the end of July the general administrator of Sandwell A.H.A. wrote to say that they were prepared to take over responsibility and the matter had been referred to a meeting of the Joint Consultative Committee to be held in September. We then made plans for closure but at their request we extended our time until the end of April 1981. We then formally closed our workshop and in due course wound up our West Bromwich subsidiary company. In the meantime, Sandwell had created a new facility in Simpson Street with equipment and premises that shone like new pins compared to the two factories where our workshops were located. Unfortunately most of our long-stay attenders did not fit the concept for rehabilitation within these pristine conditions and within a few months many of our fears were realised when all the long-stay schizophrenic patients were no longer in attendance and had been replaced by people with less severe and less challenging psychiatric problems. Most of the former attenders drifted back into the hospital run services by various routes. From the outset the West Bromwich factory had been run by a seconded All Saints Hospital charge nurse Mr. Tom Bolter, who had previously run our initial car wash in Northbrook Street. He was a man with great initiative and together with a small group of dedicated nursing assistants he created throughout its existence a splendid sheltered workshop and social club for many of the most dependent ex-patients in the community. Without his enterprise I doubt if it could have lasted as long as it did, given the difficulties it encountered but Mr. Bolter, who could be very prickly with authority when he was thwarted or perceived injustice, has to take a huge amount of the credit for the venture in West Bromwich. When Alberta Works factory closed he was approaching retirement, but until then he returned to run the car wash in Bacchus Road.

Our relations with Sandwell remained rather strained even after handover. The Treasurer of Sandwell A.H.A. anticipated that the surplus funds from W.BI.T.A. would be passed on to meet some of the costs of their new workshop. We had to point out that under Clause 7 of our Memorandum of Association any surplus from such a dissolution could be returned to the parent company and as the parent company had nurtured and supported its subsidiary since formation that was the directors' decision. It should be said that at the onset of the West Bromwich venture we had tremendous support which was sustained throughout our time there from the C.H.C. and by elected representatives and many others. By the time of closure however there had been great changes in local government and health service administration with the creation of a new borough and a new health authority. By then we were dealing with new officials who had not been around at the time we began and had not the same awareness of the problems that existed previously. Perhaps it is these ever-changing perceptions of voluntary organisations, such as B.I.T.A. during administrative changes that has seen so many of other I.T.A.s disappear over the years.

It would not be possible to leave 1980 without recording that on 9th June B.T. Davis died. I think in retrospect that he more than anyone was the founding father of B.I.T.A. He helped form it and when surrounded by enthusiasts he kept all of our feet on the ground and from the beginning insisted that we progressed on a responsible and sound financial basis. A highly successful accountant, there was much to learn from his consistent wisdom and sound advice. Although he was our financial brain he had many business interests and had the foresight to have his company right-hand man W.C.(Bill) Lea appointed a director at B.I.T.A. formation and on Bill Lea fell the responsibility for the implementation of our financial affairs. With the death of Mr. Davis, Bill Lea bore both responsibility for advice and implementation.

In the meantime, despite the efforts of the Administrative Assistant the unit run by the Employment Services Agency continued to run down in numbers, with by the end of 1980, less than twelve in attendance at any one time. Their full time DRO had been withdrawn and replaced by someone whose responsibility for referrals was part of a wider responsibility. He was spending only a few hours per week with us. Some of the workers terminated by the E.S.A. came back to work for B.I.T.A. but others who were terminated were lost, and their outcome was difficult to ascertain through the vagueness of the feedback we received in some cases. It was evident that unless there was some fundamental change in E.S.A. attitude that our collaborative project was coming to an end. Perhaps it had run its course. Perhaps it only served its purpose in those initial years of promising rehabilitees and plentiful employment. But one suspects its end was as much due to administrative reforms and changing personnel, and with new ideas that clashed with previous concepts.

As it was clear that fundamental charges were coming I asked our administrative assistant, Janice Ledbrook to produce a report on our current role and organisation and at the end of March 1981 she produced a detailed report which became a blueprint for action for the future. This report detailed the difficulties in the working relationship between ourselves and the officers at the E.S.A. but it seemed to me that there was a fundamental gap now in goals and philosophy that was unlikely to be bridged.

More importantly from a practical point of view were details of shortcomings that required attention. Among these was the need to improve the environment and as a result we embarked upon a programme of redecoration, replacement of toilets and washing facilities, improvements in heating and replacement of the fire alarm system. These were all possible in the short term from our own capital. The report also emphasised the need for a canteen, which we adopted as a longer term goal together with replacements of workbenches and chairs.

Her report also emphasised the need to improve communications with referring sources, a recurring problem, and suggestions for improving our own record system, all of which were adopted. It also emphasised now that we had a firm financial base due to the efforts of Mr. Williams that there was a need to look at ways of diversification of work and skills, and at adaptation to the problems arising from the changing economic and social climate.

It was a very clear and helpful report, which allowed us to plan for the immediate future at least. It had become very evident that we had to adapt and change to survive as a viable and useful organisation, and it is an exercise that we have repeated periodically. However despite our own plans for the future we had to regularly revise them to meet the changes elsewhere. St the beginning of 1982 we had to cope with another NHS reorganisation. The Birmingham Area Health Authority disappeared to be replaced by five new authorities in the city, North, East, South, West and Central.

The Lord Mayor Councillor John Alden with the Lady Mayoress Councillor Mrs Deidre Alden cutting the 40th Anniversary cake at the Carnival and Sports Day Event 5 July 2003.

40th Anniversary Event. The Lord Mayor Councillor John Alden and Lady Mayoress Councillor Mrs Deidre Alden pictured with BITA Chair Dr Norman Imlah, Mrs Hazel Imlah and Chief Executive Erica Barnett.

Chief Executive Erica Barnett meets the 'robot' at the 40th Anniversary Event.

Mrs Hazel Imlah presented with a bouquet of flowers by service user Carol Parsons at the 40th Anniversary Event.

40th Anniversary Event. BITA Chair Dr Norman Imlah pictured with his wife Hazel (left) and Chief Executive Erica Barnett.

The 40th Anniversary cake.

40th Anniversary Event. Gospel singers from the Kingstanding Elim Church providing live music.

*40th Anniversary Event. Final of the Tug-of-War contest between
BITA staff and service users.*

*40th Anniversary Event. Final of
the Tug-of-War contest between
BITA staff and service users.*

*40th Anniversary Event. Workshop
manager Stephen Thomas and his
wife Kay meet the 'robot'.*

40th Anniversary Event. The Lord Mayor Councillor John Alden presents a sports trophy to service user Patrick Balfour.

40th Anniversary Event. The BITA Fashion Show. Hannah Beard shows off the Mary Quant look from the 1960's.

Bhangra dancers providing entertainment at the 40th Anniversary Carnival and Sports Day Event 5 July 2003.

The front of the Digbeth premises showing the newly built retail shop with awning.

The Lord Mayor, Councillor Theresa Stewart, unveiling the plaque to commemorate the opening of the newly refurbished premises in September 2000, pictured with Chief Executive Erica Barnett.

BITA Staff team pictured on the annual staff development day at Fircroft College in July 2003.

Chief Executive Erica Barnett pictured with the 'Iron Man' candle, commissioned by Birmingham City Council in 1998.

Dr Lynne Jones MP for Birmingham Selly Oak, pictured with Chief Executive Erica Barnett and service users, prior to addressing BITA's Annual General Meeting in October 2002.

Sophia Christie Chief Executive of East Birmingham PCT presenting a certificate to a student at the St. Anne's Centre in May 2003.

The first impact on us was the resignation of John Bettinson from our Council in January. Mr. Bettinson had become involved in our affairs when he became Chair of the old Dudley Road Management Committee of which All Saints Hospital was a part, and at the previous reorganisation he had been appointed Chair of the Birmingham Area Health Authority. He decided when that was abolished not to continue in the NHS and in consequence he no longer saw himself with a role at B.I.T.A. It was a great personal regret as he was a staunch supporter and a wise counsel. The NHS loss was much greater. They could ill afford to lose men with the abundant common sense, impartiality and fairness of John Bettinson.

Reorganisation brought its own problems. From dealing with one financial officer we now found ourselves dealing with five, and sometimes with new appointees in those departments who knew nothing of our origins or relationship to the service. At a practical level we had to inform them of their need to reimburse travelling expenses of our clients, and payments for the food we provided during the day. All this took time before the various financial officers had confirmed their obligations and months elapsed before we received the payments that were due. It was as well that by this time we had sufficient cash reserves.

Our sound financial position owed much to Mr. Williams and the firm financial footing he had established through the workshop. It allowed us to be self sufficient apart from the seconding of staff for supervision and in his fifteen years he had established an industrious authentic factory, performing mainly sub-contracted work at various skill levels making increased profits which not only sustained our existence but gave us the capital to steadily improve our working environment. This progress continued despite the run down of the unit run by the Manpower Services, and when in May 1982 the E.S.A. officers produced their own report making various recommendations that we could either not agree, or not afford, or both, on Mr. Williams recommendation we agreed that the time had come for a parting of the ways. By this time there were only three people attending the E.S.A. unit while we had one hundred and seventy all fully employed in work of variable levels of skill. By this time Mr. Williams was well past the normal retirement age and at the end of April 1983 he retired. He probably remained too long as his health became indifferent toward the end, but he was very ably supported by his deputy, Mr. Underhill, who took an increasing proportion of the day to day responsibility over the last two years. In view of the enormous contribution that Mr. Williams made to the establishment of B.I.T.A., the Board who had made him a fellow director felt that he should continue until he made the decision to go and it was his decision in the end. He had been such an influence over the whole commercial side of the organisation that his departure left an end of an era effect upon us. Unlike the situation at the time of his appointment, we had no call to make an immediate decision about a replacement as we knew that his deputy could keep everything on track and so we made no immediate appointment and Mr. Underhill became acting manager while we reviewed the situation.

That situation had also been affected by the disappearance of B.T. Davis on whom we were dependent for our financial advice. The firm had continued after the death of Mr. Davies under his partners but in 1983 was taken over by another firm of accountants, Stanley & Co. This resulted in the redundancy of our director Bill Lea and the potential loss of the man who had implemented all our financial policies from the start.

As directors we were aware of the coming changes at the departure of Mr. Williams. We decided that the needs for the future required a financial secretary and that the position of administrative assistant had become largely redundant. The ending of the E.S.A section had virtually ended the liaison role, while referrals and reports records were under the direction of the seconded charge nurse. The retirement of the previous charge nurse had resulted in the secondment of Mr. John Chan as charge nurse. Hitherto the charge nurse had often seen things differently from Mr. Williams, but Mr. Chan established a much more harmonious relationship and his diplomacy and efficiency created a smoother system of care that did not interfere with working requirements.

No doubt the availability of Mr. Lea combined with the loss of our financial director influenced policy, but as we could not afford both and retaining both would have made administration top heavy, we decided with regret to make the administrative assistant redundant and replace the post with that of financial secretary.

In due course Mr. Lea was appointed financial secretary from 1st July 1983, and on taking up the post he resigned his position as a director. Not only had we solved our financial direction, but with the departure of the general manager we had in place in the main factory Mr. Lea who could be on the spot to oversee the general management until such time as we made a decision about Mr. Williams successor.

In the event I discovered that Mr. Lea and Mr. Underhill formed a very close working relationship. Consequently we resolved our problem of general manager by confirming Mr. David Underhill in the post from 1st January 1984. It provided a smooth transition to a situation, which had evolved into much more of a sheltered workshop for about 180 people. The lack of outside employment opportunities and the reduced potential of many referrals had resulted in a relatively permanent sheltered workshop population. The work itself had also become fairly standard, with four firms providing most of our sub-contracts. By far the largest contract was with G.K.N. with screw sorting varying from the simplest level of work we provided but including a more demanding product called Pozi-Drive. This was a box with eight compartments, seven of them with screws of different sizes and the eighth with a screwdriver. The plastic boxes containing these were sold by various retailers for years and all of the Pozi-Drive boxes were assembled and distributed from our factory. One of our other main contracts involved assembling sets of kitchen utensils. These came to us in bulk from the Far East, we assembled sets of them on cards for retail, and despatched them direct to retailers. A third contract involved the assembling of electrical table lamps and a fourth requiring more skill, the assembling of electrical fuses and appliances from their component parts. There were some other smaller and less regular contracts but by 1984 the workforce was relatively static and so was the work. The work had evolved partly because it was very suited to the workplace, but also because Mr. Williams had established very fair payments for our main contracts. We had established ourselves as capable of good quality control and the main firms trusted us to dispatch direct to their retail customers. This was a position which Mr. Underhill inherited and which he understood very well from working in the system. In a sense we had evolved into a large work-oriented day centre. During 1983 and 1984 all the recommended refurbishment, alterations and redecoration were completed and plans were in hand to provide a canteen. The work was sufficiently lucrative for us to be able to pay transport, meals and allowances to all our workers who were not supported from their referring authorities and that included all social service referrals and in whole or part, some of the hospital referrals, Mr. Williams had concentrated exclusively on the work aspects of our provisions, but Mr. Underhill began to develop a social dimension as well and recreations such as snooker, table tennis, darts and outings began to be introduced.

Once again the changes in the NHS brought fresh people and new organisations into the situation, and with it many who had very different perceptions of our role. During 1984 the Community Health Councils became involved and with five health authorities different groups wished to visit. Although we were independent and were not under direct C.H.C. authority we had accepted their right to be involved, but with each operating independently the question was which C.H.C.? Historically we had regarded West Birmingham C.H.C as our main contact but in 1984 Central Birmingham having discovered that our factory was in their area began to take a special interest and various members of the C.H.C., depending upon their contacts, took it upon themselves to direct various queries about us to different people in NHS management including Chairs of Boards, and we found ourselves inundated with requests to provide information so that the C.H.C. enquiries could have a reply. Fortunately the secretary of the Central C.H.C. at the time, Mr. Ian McArdle was already familiar with our work through his own involvement in a mental health charity, and after informal discussions with him I drafted a letter dealing with all the points being raised and copies of the letter were sent to the various health authorities so that they could better explain our position to their C.H.C.s. As the letter set out to explain our position in 1984 just over twenty years after our formation the letter is reproduced at the end of this chapter. In 1985 events would occur that would once again produce fundamental changes in policy.

𝔅irmingham 𝔍ndustrial 𝔗herapy 𝔏imited

Head Office & Works: 201 –206 ALCESTER STREET .
DIGBETH. BIRMINGHAM. B12 0NQ Telephone: 021-773 1455

Reply to: All Saints Hospital, Lodge Road, Birmingham. B18 5SD

OUR REF. NWI /JB   YOUR REF.   DATE   6th July 1984

Dear Mr. McArdle,

Thank you for your letter of 14th May, 1984, in my reply to my questions.

While I accept the points you make in the first paragraph, and we do not dispute the right of a Community Health Council to concern itself with an establishment which provides facilities for patients and ex-patients, we do have a problem if we have to be answerable to a number of related bodies. Whereas a particular hospital is usually visited by one C.H.C, we take patients from areas covered by several C.H.C's, and we already have official visits from West Birmingham C.H.C. and we had assumed for various reasons that this was the C.H.C. most involved. Although the factory is located in Central District, part of the B.I.T.A. is in West District. Until the recent transfer of John Conolly Hospital the number of attenders from Central Districts was very small, whereas the bulk of the attenders come from West, and then South and East Birmingham. N.H.S. staff allocated to B.I.T.A. are on the establishment of the West Birmingham Health Authority, by arrangement with the regional Health Authority, so it was natural that we assumed West Birmingham C.H.C. would feel most involved.

Having made these points, which no doubt your C.H.C. will consider, I will deal with the points raised in the report on your visit to B.I.T.A. on 25th January, 1984.

Attenders and Payments

I think it must be made clear that B.I.T.A. has never set out to pay wages. No establishment of the kind could possibly achieve the output necessary to pay normal wages. The objectives of B.I.T.A. are to provide an authentic factory-type atmosphere so that rehabilitees can work under conditions similar to ordinary industry; to negotiate rates with sub-contracting firms that do not provide firms with a cut-price rate as did most hospital based units at the time B.I.T.A. was set up. All of the money paid to B.I.T.A. is ploughed back into the organisation once running costs are met. What we do pay are incentive bonuses, according to what we can afford, and these bonuses are the same basis for each person varying according to their standard of work and application. Where the variations arise is in the payments made to the attenders by all the various agencies which refer them. All receive the basic allowances to which they are entitled (Social Security, etc.). In

Reproduction of the letter to Mr. McArdle of 6th July 1984.

addition, some receive from their referring agency the maximum allowances they can receive for work therapy, while other agencies do not pay maximum.

This is not money paid to B.I.T.A. by Health Authorities. It is money paid to patients under D.H.S.S. regulations, and if they were not attending the service provided by B.I.T.A. the Health Authority would still have to pay these and, in addition, provide work therapy. The people who are worst off are those referred from non-health services, such as Social Services, who make no additional allowance, on top of which they do not even pay bus fares so that B.I.T.A. has to subsidise their referrals by giving them travelling money. Obviously, this reduces the amount available for other purposes.

The fall in numbers is due to a number of reasons. Since industrial therapy units were started in the nineteen sixties the best of the rehabilitees were in the early referrals. With the disappearance of the better ex-long stay patient there has been an inevitable drop in the standards in terms of ability of referrals. This is not peculiar to our I.T.U. and, if you enquire, you will find that other I.T.U's are having similar problems. The biggest factor, however, is in the general unemployment situation. At one time we could practically guarantee a job for our better rehabilitees, but now it is virtually impossible to find work for ex-patients, and so many feel there is little incentive as there is nothing beyond.

I would also make the point that I do not recognise the term "B.I.T.A. patients". This is a loose phrase that has no official meaning. In fact, we do not encourage the term "patients" and we have always encouraged the use of the terms "workers" or "rehabilitees".

Activity

The activity reflects that which is available to us, and in the present economic situation we are lucky to find work and maintain our volume of work. We still receive enquires for work, but these are subject to negotiation of a proper rate. There may be a greater percentage of people on screw sorting at times, but this is because the work is constant and, as indicated, we have more referrals of the lower standard of workers than previously.

It is not our role to review each attender from a therapeutic angle. That is the role of the referring agent. Some referrers call regularly and review their referrals, but some do not. From All Saints we allocate regular sessions to a doctor who attends regularly to review our own patients. I think it is a matter of asking the various referring agencies how they review their patients.

Accommodation

First can I make a point from the previous report which states the factory is old. This is not true. The factory is not very old, and if this is thought old you should have seen the two previous factories we had to occupy and establish ourselves in. They were really old:

Reproduction of the letter to Mr. McArdle of 6th July 1984.

I agree that the absence of a canteen is a major deficiency, but we have made application for Inner City funding with support from West Birmingham Health Authority for this facility. It is in my opinion a high priority, but we do not have the resources ourselves to make this provision as we have had a considerable expenditure in the past year on toilets, floor coverings, heating and lighting, interior and exterior painting, and fire alarm replacements.

The issue of provision of a canteen was opposed by the former manager and this delayed the decision, but we would still require to be funded from an outside source whenever we decided to make the provision.

On the issue of fire precautions, the factory has always received regular visits from the fire service and the local fire officer recently inspected the factory and, subject to minor amendments, is very pleased with the fire arrangements.

Staffing and Policy

Going to the previous report, there are two groups of staff, but not two different policies. The two groups of staff are analogous to the conditions in any other organisation, namely production and personnel. In our case the production staff are told to concentrate on production irrespective of the origin of their workers. The personnel and welfare side is manned by nursing staff because we recognise the problems of our workers are much greater than in an ordinary factory and this requires the personnel side to be much more involved. It has been the philosophy to maintain a balance between the two roles for a common policy. However, all has not been perfect in this respect and we had the unsatisfactory situation for a time of differences between a former nursing officer and a former manager. This was a personality problem, not a policy problem, and as both have now retired that issue should no longer exist.

Finance

The £77,078 surplus at 31st December, 1982, does not mean that B.I.T.A. has funds approaching that sum. The word surplus is the total amounts received less the total amounts paid each year. Out of this there is the depreciation of fixed assets, additional purchase of assets and repayments of loans. Thus the surplus of £77,078 has no connection with the moneys available for payments to workers. If B.I.T.A. did not manage its finances like any other public company and pay its overheads and loans it would be out of business. It is wholly incorrect to suggest therefore, that there is any connection between the surplus sum and the bonus rates paid to rehabilitees.

I trust that this deals with the specific points to your satisfaction. I would like to make some final points. B.I.T.A. has never enjoyed substantial subsidy from the N.H.S. and on balance the N.H.S. has received far more than it has given, and Social Services, which use the facility, has never given anything. The only regular subsidy from N.H.S. funds is the

Reproduction of the letter to Mr. McArdle of 6th July 1984.

provision of supervisors, who for convenience are graded as nursing assistants, but are not nurses. If the N.H.S. did not provide this supervision they would certainly have had to provide similar supervision somewhere for the thousands of ex-patients who have gone through B.I.T.A. In fact, B.I.T.A. has provided the only major work shop facility in this city for twenty years, and had it not existed the Health Authorities would certainly have been required to make some alternative provision. In the beginning B.I.T.A. set out to be as self-supporting as possible and still has that attitude, but in economic hard time it behoves those who have the interests of ex-psychiatric patients at heart to gain more support from statutory sources if levels are to be maintained.

Of course it may be thought that organisations such as B.I.T.A. are an anachronism and have had their day. However, none of the 170 workers are under any compulsion to attend. To a great many of the hard core it is their life and the alternative, if we did not exist, could be the streets during the day. It is worth asking who else would look after our 170 attenders daily if we are not there to do so. If everybody is honest about it, nobody will look after them and they will join the many ex-psychiatric patients who live in the community, but are not receiving community care.

I am sorry there has been some delay in replying in detail, and I know that you personally have always taken a compassionate interest in B.I.T.A. While we welcome the concern of your C.H.C. I trust that this concern will be expressed constructively in supporting an organisation which may not be perfect, but has for the most part had to plough a lone furrow through various forms of hard times.

Yours sincerely

Norman W. Imlah,
Managing Director.

Mr. I. McArdle,
Secretary,
Central Birmingham Community Health Council,
2nd Floor, Ringway House,
Bull Street,
BIRMINGHAM. B4 6AF

Reproduction of the letter to Mr. McArdle of 6th July 1984.

This letter had the desired effect of promoting a great deal of support from C.H.C. members, and after further visits and exchanges of views one of the Central C.H.C. members, Mr. J.A. Hall, a retired personnel officer, joined our Board of Directors.

Dr. Alan Ogden, who has remained a director since joining the Board in 1979 has provided a contribution to our history from the perspective of Rubery Hospital, where he was a consultant psychiatrist. That contribution is appended to this chapter.

PSYCHIATRIC REHABILITATION IN SOUTH BIRMINGHAM

A personal recollection by Alan Ogden.

Rubery Hill Hospital was built in 1882 on the boundary of Birmingham with Worcestershire. It was built to relieve overcrowding at All Saints Hospital but such was the rate of accumulation of patients in those days that by 1905 it was necessary to add Hollymoor Hospital in the same area. The two hospitals functioned as one group until an enquiry set up by Enoch Powell caused them to be separated and thenceforth Rubery Hill was responsible for the southern part of Birmingham.

I joined the staff in 1970 and worked there and at Selly Oak General Hospital until I retired in 1991. A little time after that the large mental hospitals were closed one by one.

Patients had always been encouraged to work in these hospitals and they contributed to the running of the grounds, the laundry and performed many domestic tasks inside the buildings. The important difference in Industrial Therapy was that patients were paid for commercial work which was brought in and thus encouraged motivation and in many cases a route to full employment.

I came to Birmingham from Bristol where I had worked with one of the founders of Industrial Therapy, Dr. Donal F. Early so I was enthusiastic about this method of rehabilitation. At Rubery there was a prefabricated building at the side of the hospital which provided some Industrial Therapy for inpatients. This was quaintly titled "Industrial occupational therapy" and was managed by nurses as there were no Occupational therapists on the staff at that time. A few patients were conveyed to the B.I.T.A. daily but the long journey did not make it easy for the numbers to be increased.

The Regional Health Authority had set up a Rehabilitation Hospital at Malvern called St. Wulstan's and our hospital was visited regularly by their consultant Dr.

Roger Morgan to assess suitable patients for transfer. This always seemed to me a peculiar arrangement for surely patients should be rehabilitated near to their roots.

Rubery Hill was unusual in also having a Music Therapy Department which was founded by Miss Angela Fenwick.

I found B.I.T.A. more useful for outpatients and as our area of responsibility extended to Balsall Heath, now Highgate some patients did not have far to travel. After I had worked in Birmingham for a few years I was invited to join the Board of Directors of B.I.T.A. and I have been pleased to serve in this capacity to the present day.

Many of our patients with chronic mental illness were managed by depot injections of antipsychotic drugs which was an enormous medical advance. These injections could be given by the nursing staff at the B.I.T.A. which meant that patients received their treatment more reliably. I used to offer follow up at the general hospital outpatients until it dawned on me that the patients and sometimes members of staff were losing valuable time so I arranged to have a regular follow up clinic at the B.I.T.A. where an office was kindly made available for the session. This proved to be a much more effective way of following up patients.

After a large housing development was built in the 1970s at Kings Norton the Local Authority decided to build a Psychiatric Day Centre there. This was the Hawkesley Day Centre which offered rehabilitative care for a wide range of patients. The treatment there was largely based on Group therapies of various kinds but there was also a well appointed woodworking shop which was very popular with some clients. After the success of the follow up clinic at B.I.T.A. I made a similar arrangement with the managers at Hawkesley and this worked very well too.

Following changes in the catchment area we became responsible for Brandwood, Billesley and Moseley and a new set of patients could be referred to B.I.T.A. About this time the Warwick Training Centre opened and offered a completely different range of rehabilitative training.

A charity opened a Day Centre in School Road, Moseley which catered for clients with chronic and severe mental illness with a variety of disciplines including Art therapy. I was invited to become a member of the management committee there too. Thus there evolved a very wide range of rehabilitative possibilities with B.I.T.A. the mainstay for returning patients to paid employment - an ambition ever more difficult to achieve as the labour market worsened.

Alongside these day treatment centres there came a wide range of living accommodation ranging from fully supported nursing homes to self-care flats and many patients were able to return to living "in the community". Contrary to the oft-repeated misinformation I don't think any patients were discharged from hospital without proper arrangements being made for their care and accommodation.

Looking back over the past 40 years the overriding impression is of the many re-organisations of the Health Service and for much of the time a tightening of budgetary control. Much of the savings on patient care has been spent on an ever increasing bureaucracy. The types of mental illness seem to have changed and we no longer have the number of patients with traditional schizophrenia but they have been replaced by an increasing number of people who are damaged by drug abuse.

Mental illness is very debilitating and there will be a need for a caring compassionate rehabilitative network of facilities into the foreseeable future and I hope that B.I.T.A. will continue to be a part of it.

Chapter Nine

FINANCING CHANGES

Early in 1985 came the decision that was to radically change our direction fundamentally and the first major crisis to threaten our continued existence. It posed the question as to whether organisations such as our own had served their purpose and were about to become history.

The change arose with a dramatic reorganisation of our main contractor, Guest Keen and Nettlefold. The Pozi-Drive operation has already been described. Basic simple screw sorting which was once the basis of many industrial therapy hospital units when they began was now seen by many as anachronistic. However to us it still provided a base level, where, if a referral could not cope they would be unlikely to be of any use in a workshop. Our real problem however was that the well-remunerated work for GKN was providing the bulk of our workshop income and allowing us to pay sums not received from the statutory authorities. By the end of 1984 we were receiving over £50,000 per year from GKN sub-contracts.

In April 1985 we received a letter from the General Manager of GKN Fasteners of their intention to reduce the amount of work that they required. It was obvious from the letter that a reorganisation within their firm was taking place that would see the end of hand operated screw sorting and the discontinuation of their Pozi-Drive. By the end of June all work from GKN ceased and we were faced with the prospect of finding the £50,000 that the loss of their contract entailed. While some of the blame lay with us in becoming too dependent on one firm and is the kind of domino reaction that can affect many normal businesses too dependent on one source, in our case it had developed because it was available when other work was hard to find. We could not in the short term make good this loss. With our other main contractors our output was at the maximum of their requirements and in 1985 suitable sub-contract work of the kind with which we were familiar was not available. It was obviously time to change direction but the immediate requirement was a plan for financial survival. I think it was here that the goodwill we had established with the statutory authorities came to our aid.

It first became necessary to inform the relevant health district authorities of an impending problem, and if we were to close 175 people would have to be referred back for care. At the time the attendance breakdown was as follows:

South District:	24
North & East:	20
West:	65
Central:	51
Out of City:	15

This stimulated the districts to the extent that various individuals and committees came to visit, report back and make various recommendations, some very pertinent, some unrealistic and some quite ludicrous. Despite all these interventions and suggestions two crucial authorities had to be put in the picture and consulted and on their perception of our value, our future really depended.

The first of these letters was to Councillor Mrs. Theresa Stewart who was Chair of Birmingham Social Services Committee. Mrs. Stewart was already familiar with the work of B.I.T.A. and had visited our workshop. In the letter I explained the changing nature of our clientele, the service which we provided entirely free of charge up until that time to social services. I had to point out that with the loss of the G.K.N. contract we could not continue to pay social services clients their travelling and attendance allowances in the near future and without a longer term solution closure was an option. Mrs. Stewart responded positively immediately and requested the Head of Social Services Inspectorate to contact us. After doing so and consulting with the five health authorities the problem of our immediate financial position was passed to the Joint Funding Committee and in October I received a letter from Mr. A.J. Prescott to say that with the approval of the five District Management Teams we were allocated £19,000, £5,000 each from Central, West and South and £2,000 each from North and East. This together with negotiations between Mr. Lea and our bank allowed us to continue our existing commitments while we made longer-term plans.

The longer term depended predominantly on the health authorities. In August 1985 I wrote at length to Dr. Beasley the specialist in Community Medicine in the West Midlands Regional Health Authority. In fact it was a reiteration of the letter sent to Mrs. Stewart, but more detailed. In addition, I summarised the outline of the more constructive meetings we had had with the representatives of local health and social services to date. The crux of the letter however was two-fold. The first was to ask the Regional Authority if they wished our service to continue, and if so to negotiate a method of remuneration that left us less vulnerable to the external economic climate and the uncertainties of solely depending on the decisions of our commercial contractors. At the same time it was evident to us, and in our discussions that to survive long term we needed to diversify our work and provide work opportunities such as craft industries which were not purely dependent on the amount of income we received for survival.

The second point was the need for funds to keep us going while we discussed our future role. We needed more than £19,000 to maintain our existing commitments until the end of the financial year and that gap was demonstrated in an attached financial report as £25,000. Again the response was positive. Dr. Beasley arranged for relevant officers, and members of the R.H.A.s advisory committee on psychiatric rehabilitation to visit and discuss with us the way forward. At the same time the R.H.A. made us a one off payment of £25,000 pending negotiations to put us on a firmer financial basis and to agree the means by which we might widen the range of our activities.

It became evident that the large consensus of opinion was that we were a very desirable facility providing a useful and necessary service, and that our disappearance would create immense problems for health and social services which they would find it hard to replace in the short term, and only at a considerable cost. Having agreed we had a future the R.H.A. set up a working party under Mr. D. Pickup the Regional Works Manager to liaise with the various health and social services in Birmingham. In his letter to the authorities, Mr. Pickup stated that the Regional Management Team had taken a firm view that B.I.T.A. must be supported and strengthened. It proposed to meet with authorities to work out an equable system of support, a programme to expand our facilities which would depend upon the degree of support, and a basis for future management liaison between the statutory authorities and B.I.T.A. directors.

The first of a number of crucial meetings between the R.H.A. working party and ourselves represented by Mr. Lea, Mr. O'Leary and myself took place on 13th February 1986. At that meeting the existing system of payments between the statutory authorities and B.I.T.A. was outlined as follows:

Nursing and Supervision

The R.H.A. had arranged from 1969 onwards for Dudley Road H.M.C. to pay for 10 nursing assistant grade supervisors to work at B.I.T.A. The cost of this was reimbursed to Dudley Road H.M.C. by the R.H.A. top slicing the budget of those other H.M.C.s with referrals to B.I.T.A. West Birmingham Health District had taken over this responsibility from the former Dudley Road H.M.C. In addition a charge nurse and nursing assistant were seconded from All Saints Hospital to manage the nursing supervision and provide personnel and welfare services. These were paid for by West Birmingham from nursing budgets.

Transport

B.I.T.A. had a contract with West Midlands Passenger Transport Authority for transport of attenders in West Birmingham. B.I.T.A. paid the Transport Authority monthly and recovered the cost annually from West Birmingham Health Authority.

Each month B.I.T.A. paid the travelling expenses of attenders from Midland Nerve, Highcroft, Hollymoor, Rubery and John Connolly Hospitals and was reimbursed monthly by those hospitals.

B.I.T.A. pays the travelling expenses of referrals by Social Services without reimbursement.

Meals

Hollymoor and All Saints provide sandwiches daily. B.I.T.A. provides sandwiches for all the other hospitals which then reimburse the costs monthly. Patients referred by Social Services and from various lodging houses who did not bring packed lunches had these supplied by B.I.T.A. without reimbursement.

Allowances

The allowances to attenders for their work was paid or reimbursed as follows;
Rubery Hill and John Connolly (Central) - paid 100%
All Saints (West) - 50% paid by West and 50% paid by B.I.T.A.
Midland Nerve and Highcroft – All allowances paid
Hollymoor and Social Services – only by B.I.T.A.

This demonstrated a very variable level of commitment and a confusing mixture of systems of payment that was unequal across the service. There was a requirement to resolve these anomalies and devise some unified system.

Various other points emerged at that meeting. Among them was the desire at B.I.T.A. to look at ways of extending the range of work to a more creative type of activity which would also be remunerative. There was also a wish to extend the social functions and social amenities and introduce programmes to develop social and domestic skills. There was a need for a better liaison between social services in particular, but also with some of the referring doctors and nurses over referrals welfare and placement. It was pointed out that B.I.T.A. staff, in particular the seconded charge nurse, spent a lot of time on sorting out allowance matters in default of anybody else dealing with these. There was also a recognition of the need to continue to improve the facilities at B.I.T.A., and in particular to make changes to accommodate the proposed new ventures on the premises, or outside if necessary.

The various meetings continued with the next significant development on 24 June 1986 when all the B.I.T.A. directors met with the West Midlands R.H.A. working party. Although progress was being made social services had financial constraints and each Health Authority was, on request, participating in a multi-disciplinary review of all their people attending B.I.T.A. This was taking time and in order to allow this, Mr. Pickup announced that the R.H.A. would continue its financial support, following the expiry of the initial payment, until April 1987.

It was also agreed that two people nominated by the R.H.A., one from health and one from social services should become directors of B.I.T.A. and the **B.I.T.A.** Board welcomed that proposal. In due course Mr. Peter Summers, Regional Nurse for Special Care Projects was nominated to represent the R.H.A. and Mr. L. Bayfield from Central District Social services to represent Social services. They were duly elected to the B.I.T.A. board at its A.G.M. in October 1986. In fact, Louis Bayfield did not serve as a director because he was a local government officer, and advised that it was inappropriate. However he attended board meetings as an advisor for a time. Subsequently Mr. Barry Thornton was nominated as Social Services representative and served as a full and committed director.

In September 1986 Mr. Lea informed us that he intended to retire at the end of October due to his failing health and he intended to live in Wales with his son. Mr. Lea had administered our finances from formation and he was greatly missed. He was a quiet but meticulously efficient man, like all good accountants, and his leaving left a gap. On Mr. Lea's recommendation, Olive Underhill was appointed Company Secretary. Olive had run our office with great efficiency since 1967 but lacked the experience of the trained accountant. For this we sought the help from Stanley & Co. who had taken over the firm of B.T. Davis, and in particular one of their directors Mr. Peter Beddard. He has remained an invaluable advisor to the Association until the present day, continuing the financial guidance that began with Mr. Davis and Mr. Lea.

Meantime our meetings with statutory authorities continued and became protracted, partly due to delays by some of the authorities in completing surveys, and partly because some authorities had alternative solutions that were more pipe dreams than reality, as it became clear that the money for their proposed new ventures was not available. At the meeting in June 1986 the R.H.A. had before it recent research work carried out by Dr. Helen Barnes at B.I.T.A. In that survey she showed that many currently attending at the time had very little support other than that which they received at B.I.T.A. and that most of them were very satisfied with their care, and would be virtually destitute of any support if the services at B.I.T.A. were not available.

Some authorities were happy to accept the findings of Dr. Barnes and did not consider it necessary to duplicate assessments. However some, notably from Social Services wanted to pursue their own concepts but the Regional Board working party came to the conclusion that these alternatives were theoretical and idealistic, and did not provide a practical answer to the needs of the population they were looking at. They concluded that these were best met by the realistic approach provided at B.I.T.A. They decided that in the short to medium term at least this was the best option of care available, and in consequence the Regional Board working party gave its firm support to B.I.T.A. as a valuable community resource which must be supported.

In the meantime at B.I.T.A. efforts were being made to find alternative work to replace the lost contracts from G.K.N. and as a result of those efforts at the end of 1986 it was possible to reduce the Regional Board payment by £8,000.

Having reached these conclusions for the remainder of 1987 and into 1988 negotiations were directed to finding a direct and equable means of remuneration to B.I.TA.from statutory authorities based on a per capita attendance from each. It did mean an end to the system where anybody who was referred and was suitable was taken on. Now they could only be taken on if the relevant authority was prepared to pay for their care or rehabilitation. In December 1987 the R.H.A. working party met with representatives from the health authorities and social services. It detailed the progress made as follows;

1. Promulgating a better understanding of B.I.T.A. services and general goodwill and support.
2. Strengthening the B.I.T.A. Board with the acceptance on the Board of Directors of a Director from Region and an observer/advisor from Social Services.
3. Gaining acceptance of the role B.I.T.A. played and the need for that role to continue within an indispensable organisation with informal links to Health and Social services and with support from them.

They then set out the areas in which there had been little progress as follows:

1. In gaining material support from Social Services in view of the Social Services financial position.
2. In obtaining an understanding of a planning framework of joint care across all districts which would relate to B.I.T.A.

The conclusions of that meeting were as follows:

1. B.I.T.A. continues to be supported financially and with therapeutic input.
2. A discernable framework be developed by U.G.M.s and linked to Social Services with which B.I.T.A. is seen to continue to supply a valuable service in the independent sector.

3. A meeting be convened of Birmingham U.G.M.s with a view to furthering the aims and objectives of 1. and 2, take into account discussions with B.I.T.A., and report back to the Regional Group.

The discussions continued throughout 1988 for a suitable arrangement. In 1988 Mr. Pickup retired and his place chairing the working party was taken by his successor at region, Mr. John Knott. Mr. Pickup had worked hard on our behalf and had shown an understanding of the needs of our attenders that was much more insightful than those shown by more professionally involved personnel in some of the many meetings held with the various health and social service groups.

In October 1988 one of our directors, Mr. Hal Cohen announced his retirement. Then in his eighties, Mr. Cohen had become Chairman of All Saints Hospital Management Committee in succession to Mr. Haynes in 1964 and took the place of Mr. Haynes on the B.I.T.A. Board. He remained throughout a great support to the Association. Mr. Cohen was a dentist by profession, but gave a great deal of his time to public service with no political affiliations. He was very fair and unprejudiced, and over the years I found him an immense source of unbiased common sense. He had one unusual claim to fame. He was a keen cricketer who had a fine collection of cricket memorabilia which attracted a lot of press attention when they were auctioned upon his death. Apart from myself, he was the last remaining director of those initial ventures in 1964.

At last in June 1988 I received a letter from Mr. Knott stating that agreement had been reached that B.I.T.A. would charge District Health Authorities for the services it provided. It was also agreed that the minimal contract period be for two years with a roll on every year. Social Services were to be advised that they were to be charged for services on a similar basis, although it was thought that some of their referrals might have to be reprocessed through the relevant health authority as it was unlikely Social Services would pay for all its current clients.

The amount to be charged had still to be worked out but a meeting was held on 12 July between B.I.T.A. directors and Regional Board officers to finalise agreement in principal. Following that meeting the D.H.A.s were advised that charging for services would come into effect in April 1990. I then wrote to all the authorities that we were ready to open negotiations with authorities over the level of service to be provided and the cost. As each authority would be purchasing different numbers of places based on current attendance and estimated future needs it was necessary to meet with each separately. However Region advised authorities that in the event of no agreement being reached with a user authority the Association would have to invoice the authority at the level they considered appropriate. In the meantime we prepared packages of the services we were prepared to offer. At the same time Mr. Beddard was asked to work out the costs of providing these services based on a total of 150 clients. All calculations assumed a 50 working weeks a year of 5 days each week.

The costs took in the following: Attenders' allowances, travelling expenses, wages and national insurance of B.I.T.A. staff, rent and insurances, heat and power, telephone and post, motor and travel, bank charges, repairs to premises and plant, laundry, food and beverages, professional fees and depreciation. Initially we did not include the supervisory seconded nursing staff but after further discussion it was agreed to include these so that their costs could be proportionally divided. The current seconded staff from West Birmingham would continue but B.I.T.A. would pay in full for their salaries. It was agreed also that the arrangement of seconded staff should be phased out, and as they retired, left the service, or returned to their seconding health authority they would be replaced by staff directly employed by B.I.T.A. This would apply not only to the workshop supervisory staff, who were unqualified nursing assistants, but also to the two trained nursing staff who currently provided supervision, but mainly dealt with referrals, liaison with referrers, and the nursing and welfare needs of clients. As the workshop supervising staff were replaced they would then become responsible only to the general manager.

In return for the charges to be paid by the health authorities we proposed to provide a total day care facility based initially upon the current work therapy but in due course to be expanded to provide educational and recreational facilities. The ultimate aim, where possible, would be work and social skills therapy leading to a full return to the community. Realistically for many this full return would not be possible but clients would be retained for as long as they benefited from attendance.

More specifically we provided the following;

1. Full supervision during the hours of attendance.
2. An oversight of each attenders social and welfare needs plus any action or referral when required.
3. General clinical supervision with regular contact with the relevant community worker or team.
4. Provision of a mid-day meal and beverages for breaks.
5. The creation of leisure outlets during attendance hours and extending these to specific activities outside hours.
6. Individual social skills deficits to be assessed and given attention.

The proposals meant that the provision of service would be funded entirely by the per capita charge, and that the additional income generated by the Association from its work contracts would be utilised to fund the expansion of the facilities and the range of therapies on offer. These expansions were envisaged as increases in recreational facilities, extension of the range of work experience, provision of more classes to improve individual social skills and an improvement of facilities within the main factory. The latter included extension of canteen facilities and the creation of shower and bathing areas.

By the end of November 1989 agreement on costs and conditions were completed. It remained to negotiate with each health authority and social service the number of places they were prepared to purchase. Although costs were based on 150 we had more than that number in attendance and it was implicit in the costing procedure that purchase of places over the 150 could make a reduction in the per capita payments. Some of the subsequent negotiations were protracted and not unexpectedly those authorities with the highest number of attenders were those most quickly in agreement. An arranged number with Social Services took considerable time. Over the years a number of attenders had been loosely categorised as Social Services but the origins of their referral and whether they had ever been under Social Services was obscure. Some attenders had returned to Birmingham from outlying centres such as St. Wulstans and no longer lived in the area of original catchment. Others had drifted into the city to live after referrals from hospitals outside the city such as Barnsley Hall in Bromsgrove and St. Matthews in Burntwood. It was obvious that we could not reject any of these long-term attenders but understandable that some authorities questioned why they were now their responsibility. The greatest burden inevitably fell on West Birmingham which was severely affected by the drift of people with chronic psychoses from suburban areas into the parts of the city with high numbers of lodging houses and after-care homes. Handsworth in particular had become an area with a very high proportion of such homes, all of them coming into existence following the discharges from the city's psychiatric hospitals from 1960 onwards. Many of the people who ended up in these homes of varying quality, some good but some not so good, had never lived in the area before, but were from the outlying suburbs of the city or even from places outside the city. The process of drift of chronic psychiatric patients had been well demonstrated in the United States in the 1930's in cities such as Chicago, and later in Britain but the extent of the drift in those studies was nothing compared to the drift toward Handsworth and Aston and areas around them in the twenty five years from 1960.

It was inevitable that some negotiations were protracted but by the end most of the agreed figures purchased approximated closely to the accepted numbers currently attending, although at the end we were left with a small group whom nobody accepted belonged to them and we had no alternative but to continue to care for on our own resources. They had all been with us for a long time, and most of them were among our more productive workers who for various reasons had little hope of outside employment at that time. Negotiations were probably hardest with Social Services but even so we eventually reached an agreed number of purchased places.

By the time these arrangements were completed and put into operation in April 1990 we had made the biggest transformation since our formation. We were still dependent on selling our services but now our continued existence was no longer dependent on these, but dependent instead on a continuing need by authorities to purchase the services we were offering them. It was evident from our discussions that there were few firm or realistic plans to provide our kind of rehabilitation elsewhere so there was every likelihood that, provided we continued to deliver these services, we would be needed into the foreseeable future.

It was also evident that we had to plan changes for the future. Our income from the workshop was still vital for our growth and development but that development would require us to change our emphasis in the direction of training and at the same time take note of the changing nature of the type of work available outside.

Chapter Ten

DEVELOPMENT OF
WARWICK TRAINING CENTRE

It was probably inevitable that the new charging system would have initial difficulties and much of 1990, after its introduction in April, was spent resolving problems with the purchasing authorities. West Birmingham District, for example, had by virtue of its numbers attending, to purchase the highest number of 52 places. In attempts to balance their own budget they suggested, once the scheme was running, that if they reduced the attendance of their clients from 5 to 4 days per week they would only require to pay the equivalent of 41 places. It had to be pointed out that the costs were based on a total of 150 places and if that number was not met the per capita costs would have to increase accordingly. More importantly most of their clients would have been disadvantaged by having nowhere to go on the fifth day, would lose their payment of allowances for that day, and none of them wanted to reduce their attendance. It was one of the agreements with the Regional Board that no clients would be disadvantaged by the charges. A further point was that the provision was still subsidised by earnings in the workshop and these would drop accordingly with the drop in attendance. When these facts were pointed out West District accepted the position and paid accordingly but two of the health districts had still not paid their purchased places six months after the system was in operation, and were still questioning the basis on which payments were calculated. It was only when our accountants provided them with a full breakdown of the negotiated agreement and emphasised the cash flow problems that their non-payments were creating that we resolved the payment issue. Social Services payment in contrast went smoothly once we had reached an agreed number of places, the only problem being that the final numbers were less than the listed referrals on our books but this was inevitable given the obscure sources of original referrals. One of the great recurring problems has always been the movement of community workers within the frequent organisational changes inside the health and social services so that referring agents and the referring agency disappears leaving the client with no attachment except to ourselves.

Gradually these teething difficulties were resolved after much correspondence but 1990 saw another very significant initiative for our future development. It began when David Blakemore who was Adult Programme Coordinator at the city's Economic Development Department met with Peter Imlah, who by virtue of his position in West Birmingham had assumed responsibility for the nursing input to B.I.T.A. This was in succession to Mr. Chan who had left the health service to run his restaurant in Station Street, The New Happy Gathering.

The Economic Development Department had responsibilities for improving the training and employment opportunities available to people with disabilities. It also had a strategy which allowed it to set up pilot initiatives in pursuit of that responsibility. It was evident that in the field of mental health E.D.D. and B.I.T.A. had common grounds and David Blakemore and Peter Imlah saw the potential value of close collaboration and together put forward proposals to B.I.T.A. directors for a pilot scheme in our premises. Sarah Crawley working in E.D.D. was seconded to the B.I.T.A. for three weeks to review potential clients currently attending B.I.T.A. Sarah Crawley and Peter Imlah then visited a number of different training projects around the Midlands and as a result a paper was produced outlining an initial pilot training scheme for September 1990.

This was the beginning of what has become our Warwick Training Centre based on the floor above the main workshop and in the part of the building which occupies Warwick Street off Alcester Street, hence its eventual name. The success of the initial pilot scheme led to developments supported by E.D.D. which will be detailed as they evolve in our history. Both Sarah Crawley and Peter Imlah moved on from the posts they were in when this training initiative began, but both are now directors of B.I.T.A.

Our links with E.D.D. have continued until the present day. Their initial research suggested that up to one third of clients attending B.I.T.A. could benefit from employment training. It was agreed that this would have to be phased in, but initially there was a need for capital to develop the area into a training centre. The upper floor where Warwick Training Centre is situated had been used as a storage area in the main but leant itself well to their proposed purpose. In 1991, with support from E.D.D. an Inner City Partnership Grant of £50,000 was obtained to make the necessary transition to a training centre. The former storage floor had independent access from Warwick Street and was connected by stairs to the main workshop. In June 1991 David Blakemore wrote to advise us that the capital grant had been approved, and that additional funding was being sought for clerical support and running costs. The contract for the capital work was awarded to R.T.S. Interiors in August 1991.

On completion of the capital project the training unit had what was described as "high quality well-resourced accommodation, including a training kitchen, a computer room and an open learning centre". There were facilities for practising social and interpersonal skills, job search and career guidance. Literacy and Numeracy skills were provided within the open learning centre.

Begun in October 1990, the E.D.D. training division offered four initial access programmes on site. These were delivered by Adult Education Tutors funded through Employment Training. The clients who attended were given a comprehensive assessment, career counselling and guidance, and various other skills as appropriate.

Each training course had no more than eight participants. The new centre had a capacity for about twenty-four trainees. Progression routes for trainees included moving on to further training, sheltered placement and employment. There had been a fifty percent progression into further training and that was regarded as a high rate for the particular client group.

By early 1992 we were ready for an official opening, and on 5th February 1992 the Warwick Training Centre was officially opened by Councillor Jane Slowey. We had prepared new brochures setting out the various services available both within and outside the training centre, and including a substantial development of social and recreational facilities. We set out also our immediate future aims, which included a continuing close liaison with E.D.D. in the training area.

The official opening was well attended by professionals and managers from the health and local authorities. Our only hitch was a last minute dash to change the name on the opening plaque as another prominent local councillor had accepted the original invitation to open the centre, and when he pulled out at the last stage Councillor Slowey deputised.

By the time of the opening we were able to announce further extensive capital developments. Thanks to the efforts of Mr. Blakemore and E.D.D. further Inner City Partnership Grants for capital developments of £50,000 per year had been obtained for the next three years plus a revenue commitment of £31,000 per year for three years to staff and maintain training developments in the initial stages.

In my welcoming address on behalf of B.I.T.A. at the official opening of the Warwick Training Centre, the recent developments with E.D.D. were recognised; "because many of those who attend B.I.T.A. have special training and learning needs, and their chances of survival in the community can only be greatly enhanced by the impact of this expertise. We at B.I.T.A. have been very encouraged by the positive support from E.D.D. and thank David Blakemore, Sarah Crawley and their staff for invaluable contributions. We show in a unique way how a registered charity may collaborate closely with a statutory body in providing comprehensive care for a very needy, underprivileged section of our society".

It was also an opportunity to acknowledge the support over the years from Birmingham City Council. So the welcome concluded with; "Over the years we have had invaluable individual help from members of Birmingham City Council. In the beginning Alderman Denis Thomas, the Chairman of Public Works was enormously helpful in finding us suitable premises. During the nineteen seventies Councillor Frank Carter, the Chairman of the Social Services Committee, was a director and always took a keen interest in the activities of the Association. Our present premises, which we now own, were purchased with support from Birmingham City Council. It is therefore entirely appropriate that one of the leading members of the present Council should open this centre today, and we welcome Councillor Jane Slowey".

David Blakemore left E.D.D. in June 1992, but in a short time we owed him much for his contributions. Before he left we had drawn up plans for the capital developments over the next three years. These included;

In year one (1992-1993): the provision of new or upgraded toilet and working facilities for both sexes to complement the new training area. Removal of disused boilers to create more space for training and the development of some area for recreational and leisure activities.

In year two (1993-1994): The entrance area, off Alcester Street, to be upgraded to improve image, with a reception area, and to improve clinic treatment and personnel facilities moved down from the second floor. The second floor conversion to provide seminar rooms for training and group meetings.

In year three (1994-1995): The area designated canteen to be upgraded and combined with a training area for the development of catering and food handling skills.

In addition B.I.T.A. from its own capital planned to concurrently upgrade the main factory area with improvement of workbenches and seating and in the following year to upgrade staff toilets.

These exciting proposals all began in 1992, which is remembered as one of the key years in our history. Before leaving 1992 one or two other events are worthy of recall. In February 1992 Olive Underhill, our office manager and now company secretary completed twenty-five years employment with the Association, the first employee to do so. She had been an invaluable mainstay in the Association throughout the years. By the end of the year, David Underhill had also completed twenty-five years.

Then in August 1992 Mr. Peter Townley, a businessman with existing voluntary interests in mental health, joined the Board. This was a welcome development as we had lacked a director with specific industrial management experience since the departure of Mr. Kirk, and had become very reliant on our general managers for this aspect of our activity. Mr. Townley continues to chair our Business and Development Sub-Committee.

Early in 1993 I began a series of meetings with fellow directors Peter Townley and Peter Summers to look at our future management structure. The growth of the organisation since the training development was making it too unwieldy to control through the normal Directors' Committee meetings and at the same time there was a need to get all directors more involved. We submitted a plan for three sub-committees each with its own chair and with every director involved with at least one sub-committee. These sub-committees introduced in 1993 evolved into the present Business and Development, Training and Personnel Committees in existence today. Each committee sets its own agenda and reports to each quarterly meeting of the full committee. Once they were established we added a fourth, Finance Sub-Committee of the Association Chairman and the Chairs of the three Sub-Committees. While these were the main recommendations to come from our meetings we looked at various other matters under the general heading of aims, objectives and directions as well as future structure. We thought that social activities should continue to be encouraged but rather than incorporate them into the care programmes they might be better developed through the creation of a social club. We also looked at the way in which we might develop satellite work units both on and off site. The latter had formed part of our ongoing plans with E.D.D. and the concept of creating social firms which would employ the more skilled of our trainees had been suggested. This was a path we were prepared to explore. Part of the revenue funding obtained by E.D.D. from Inner City Partnership was to fund for three years a Business Development and Training Manager who would not only oversee Warwick Training but be responsible for starting up new work initiatives separate from the sub-contracts in our workshop.

The only off-site work at the time was still our car wash in Bacchus Road but by the end of 1993 the car wash was due for closure as the land was required for development and the lease was up by the terms of our agreement. We decided that automation had overtaken the usefulness of our hands on car wash and with dwindling numbers it was decided for economic reasons not to start a third car wash. Most were against continuing a car wash for other reasons as the climate of opinion on what constituted suitable work was changing and for both reasons it was discontinued. This did not detract in any way from its value when we began, or the funds it provided to initiate our wider concepts.

We set about obtaining our training and development officer and found, as we did for our general managers, that there were few laid down criteria of qualifications for this type of post. In September 1993 we appointed Mr. John O'Leary to the position after a series of interviews. He took up his position on 4th October, and while the training aspects of the job were partially in place through the work of E.D.D., the business development aspect was a fairly blank page for his own initiatives.

In 1993 we set in motion attempts to purchase the leasehold area of our premises. We always had part of it freehold and on the advice of Mr. Beddard we agreed that it would now make sense to purchase the rest, but negotiations were protracted and it took some time to achieve our objective.

During this same period yet another reorganisation within the health services meant another round of negotiations. In particular, our seconded staff were now employees of North Birmingham Mental Health Trust and after a series of meetings it was agreed that seconding should continue with B.I.T.A. paying the salaries of the seconded staff. However a number of these were now on the brink of retirement and it was reaffirmed that as each seconded worker retired or left they would be replaced by our own appointed staff.

In December 1993 E.D.D. gave notice of a change in our working agreement to take effect from 31st March 1994. The Warwick Training Centre had been in existence over two years with a steering group from B.I.T.A., E.D.D., Social Services, Warwick Training Centre staff and two users of the services at B.I.T.A. That group had oversight of financing, training provision, staffing and maintenance. The capital redevelopments had been completed apart from a final £50,000, due on 1st April 1994.The revenue monies had funded the Training and Business Development Manager and an administrative assistant.

From 31st March 1994 it was proposed that E.D.D. would withdraw its day-to-day support of the manning of Warwick Training and the centre develop its own organisational structure to continue to provide education, training and employment opportunities for people with mental health problems. Various alternatives were proposed from E.D.D. on the form this future structure might take but the one which the B.I.T.A. directors considered most appropriate was the full incorporation of Warwick Training Centre into B.I.T.A. with the maintenance of the education, training and employment role as set out in the grant aid conditions.

Before leaving the events of 1993 I had the opportunity as part of the process of working with the reorganised health services of showing Dr. Jennie Bywater who was the Senior Commissioning Manager for Mental Health around B.I.T.A. and discussing our past and future role. She asked how many of our clients had been readmitted to hospital while attending B.I.T.A. Without knowing the actual figure I thought it must be very few but subsequently from reliable records available to me I found that in the twelve years prior to 1993 only five people required to be readmitted to hospital, and of these three of the five were pre-planned for the purpose of reviewing and changing medication under supervision.

During 1994 most of our activity involved a completion of the capital programme of alteration, and improvements, the development of the various training programmes, and the creation of new business developments. The purpose of the latter was to create work that had a higher skill level with two main purposes. One was to provide skills based training, linked to N.V.Q.'s and opportunities for employment. The second was, at the same time, to create a business venture within the Association, which might generate income, and, if sufficiently successful, could develop into a kind of social firm, providing its own employment opportunities.

It was part of the role of the new Training and Business Development Manager to look at ways in which this might be achieved. He looked at a range of crafts and skills both in the city, and outside and the most promising of these, which he recommended was candle making. The Board accepted this proposal, the necessary skills trainers were recruited and Warwick Candles, as it came to be christened, was launched experimentally in a room at the front of the building in April 1994. Its value as a skills training facility was quickly apparent and hopes were entertained that it could become a viable enterprise. With the decision taken to give this development our support the candle making was moved to a former packing area at the back of the factory, with the general manager responsible for commercial production, and the capital plans to include a purpose-built candle making workshop complete with extractor fans. That workshop eventually opened in May 1995 with great optimism for its future. It remains a very valuable skill-training course, but after a number of attempts to get it going commercially it has not succeeded, even with skilled advisors and operatives. Our experience with Warwick Candles has placed doubts, in our view, whether social firms of this kind can become commercially viable without continued subsidised support. Our first experience with it as a commercial venture was perhaps an omen. Mr. O'Leary obtained a very promising order right at the beginning of our commercial launch only to learn that the firm giving him the order went into liquidation a few weeks later. It is probably a field which has become over competitive but Warwick Candles continues to exist for skills training and for small scale production orders, or sales at crafts fairs, but no longer with the commercial aspirations that were first envisaged.

In September 1994 the director of E.D.D. produced a report upon the training provision, by then well established at B.I.T.A. As well as detailing the capital developments, he reported that Warwick Training Centre provides, "vocation guidance and counselling, pre-vocational training, National Vocational Qualifications (NVQ) training, basic skills and English as a second language support, social skills development, work placement and progression into further training and employment. The business development workshop provided skill based training, linked to NVQ's. In 1993-94 B,I,T,A, provided vocational guidance and counselling and training for eighty-three people".

In November 1994 we lost our first Business Development Manager when John O'Leary left to fulfil a long held ambition to become a policeman. His legacy at B.I.T.A. is Warwick Candles.

There were two significant developments in 1995. In September of that year we finally completed the purchase of the outstanding freehold. The search for the relevant documents had protracted the matter but the persistence of our solicitors Stannard & Co. concluded on 21st September with the signing of the purchase documents. The cost of the outstanding freehold was £29,672.03.

Earlier in 1995 Olive and David Underhill announced their intention to both retire at the end of March 1996. Both had been with B.I.T.A. over twenty-five years and held the two key positions within the Association of Company Secretary and General Manager respectively. Olive's health had become poor and David also had recently overcome health problems so that their intention to retire was not unexpected. However they had become so much the dominant figures within B.I.T.A. that their joint departure was a major event in our history. Not only had they both fulfilled their positions with dedication and diligence, they had become deeply involved in the welfare and social activities of the client group. David in particular had promoted sporting contests and competitions with prizes for events such as snooker, darts and table tennis. They promoted various social functions for special events such as Christmas and birthdays so that their departure meant much more than just two vacancies to be filled.

The early notice of their impending retirement gave the Board time to re-evaluate their roles. It had become evident that the nature of rehabilitation was changing and although we retained the term industrial it was now in a very general sense and not in the narrow context when we began. Industry was changing rapidly and so was the type of work available. The old industrial workshop was no longer the central core of our activity. The development of the Warwick Training Centre, with its various courses including computer training, and the desire to create skills training as we were doing with candle making and leaded windows was widening the scope of our operations. Although some of our directors began to feel that some of our sub-contracted work was anachronistic, it still represented jobs that somebody had to do and still served the dual purpose of providing work training and income. It was not that its day was over, but only that it had now a less central part in our activities.

It was not only the expansion with which we were concerned. With the gradual retirement of NHS seconded staff (two during 1995) we were employing more people directly responsible to us, involving our own pension and bonus schemes. On top of these there was the growing staff in Warwick Training, plus the question of employing the tutors for the programmes. The latter was to provide on-going problems while we attempted to resolve the best form of relationship with our tutors.

With these and other issues, such as the need for ongoing negotiations with changing management systems within the NHS and Social Services, we considered that the day of the general manager predominantly responsible for obtaining suitable sub-contracted orders, and ensuring a regular production line, was in the past. That was still an essential role in our future, but we needed a much broader based manager who in effect would assume the role of Chief Executive and be given that title.

At our Board of Directors meeting in October 1995 we met officially to resolve the future management structure and agreed to appoint a Chief Executive with overall responsibility to the non-executive Board for running all aspects of B.I.T.A. It was agreed that Mr. Summers would prepare a job description for Board approval and that the post be advertised as soon as possible, so that the person appointed was ready to take up the post by the time David and Olive Underhill retired.

We had forty-four applications for the position and in February 1996 we interviewed a short list of six candidates. The outcome was the appointment of Erica Barnett as our Chief Executive and she took up her appointment on the retirement of Olive and David Underhill at the end of March 1996.

The appointment of Erica Barnett was a complete departure from the background of our three general managers to date. She was a university graduate who had been a Service Manager with the Citizens' Advice Bureau for sixteen years before accepting our invitation to become our Chief Executive. Our decision to change direction in our management was considered bold, even risky by some of our directors and staff, but the time had come for a transition. In the early history of B.I.T.A. it had gone through a number of distinct phases, which have simply reflected the changing phases in society and for us in particular, the management of mental health. The key to any success we have had has been to recognise change and adapt to meet those changes.

In the beginning we were a community based rehabilitation unit assisting in the return of many former long-stay patients to employment. When that initial period ran its course we became more of a sheltered workshop in the community, providing work, recreation and support for a more disabled former long-stay population. When the large psychiatric hospitals were rapidly closed, and the gradual shift to Care in the Community suddenly became a flood, and we received many more of a new type of referral we needed to change again. The revised system of payments from statutory authorities, the development of Warwick Training, the attempt to create potential social firms such as Warwick Candles and the need to look at different types of work made it essential to make this change in direction. Erica Barnett is still our Chief Executive. The next chapter belongs to her and she has agreed to write her contribution to our history.

The main workshop at Digbeth. The contact customer provided T-shirts for workers.

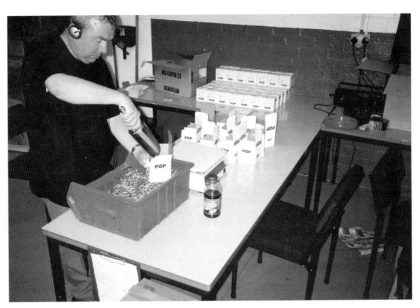

One of the weighing and packing jobs from a contract customer.

Assembling rivets in the Digbeth workshop for a contract customer.

An compressed air-operated machine acquired at the Digbeth workshop in the late 1990's. Used to press clips to bolts for use in the construction industry.

Some of the electrical wiring work done regularly in the Digbeth workshop in the mid 1990's.

User Group Chair David Powell wearing his World Mental Health Day T-shirt with another member of the users group.

A foot operated stapling machine, newly acquired for use in the Digbeth workshop in 2002.

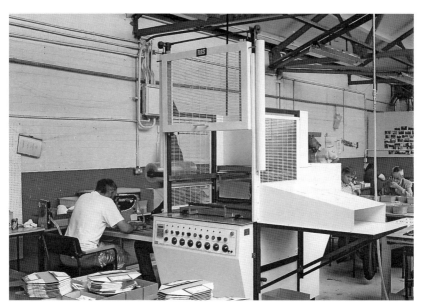

An air press operated machine used for skin packing work in many industries. Newly acquired for use in the Digbeth workshop in 2002.

The Investors in People plaque awarded in March 2000.

(right) Plaque commemorating the opening of the newly refurbished premises by The Lord Mayor, Councillor Theresa Stewart in September 2000.

THESE REFURBISHED PREMISES WERE OFFICIALLY OPENED BY THE RIGHT WORSHIPFUL, THE LORD MAYOR OF BIRMINGHAM COUNCILLOR THERESA STEWART ON 26 SEPTEMBER 2000

(left) A plaque commemorating the opening of the Warwick Training Centre in February 1992 by Councillor Jane Slowey.

(right) Plaque commemorating the capital grant support from the National Lottery Charities Board in 2000.

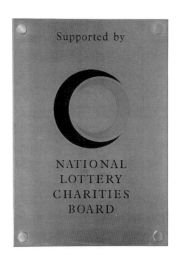

Dr Jenny Bywaters Senior Commissioning Manager at Birmingham Health Authority unveiling the Investors in People plaque in March 2000.

The Lord Mayor, Councillor Theresa Stewart, touring the Digbeth workshop with Chief executive Erica Barnett in September 2000.

Celebration of Achievement April 1998. Lord (Roy) Hattersley presenting students with certificates.

The Lord Mayor, Councillor Theresa Stewart, presenting certificates to students at the AGM in September 2000.

World Mental Health Day 1998. Staff and service users at the stall outside Boots in the city centre.

The Warwick Candles team of candlemakers pictured in April 1998.

Chapter Eleven

FROM 1996 INTO THE 21ST CENTURY

In April 1996 I was appointed as the Association's first Chief Executive. The post was created by the Board of Directors following a major review of the organisation's activities and in light of the impending retirement of the General Manager David Underhill and the Office Manager/Company Secretary Olive Underhill who had both been with BITA for many years.

I came into post at a time of great change in the way that mental health services were being delivered across Birmingham by the two mental health trusts. The Association needed as a priority to engage in meaningful discussions with senior trust managers about the way in which we could work in partnership with them.

Equally importantly we needed to convince our main funding body, the Birmingham Health Authority that the organisation was in a good shape to continue delivering services to the standards they required. Monitoring and evaluation were becoming a pre-requisite for continued funding and it was necessary to put in place the infrastructure to facilitate those systems. To that end, my first few months in post were spent assessing the needs of the organisation in terms of administration, finance, technology, recruitment and selection, staff training and development. Policies and procedures were developed and implemented around all these and many more areas.

Some minor refurbishment was agreed by the Board of Directors which authorised the release of £15000 from the reserves. This allowed me to move the canteen from an open area of the workshop, creating a partitioned Games Room in its place. The full size snooker table, much loved by the former general manager, was carefully moved into the new games room. The new canteen was separate from the workshop with a proper kitchen which met health and safety requirements and provided a more congenial environment for service users to have their breaks. The workshop was painted a bright blue and yellow, the floor was re-painted and the whole environment was much improved.

The Association was generally held in some high esteem by mental health practitioners and we continued to receive referrals from across the city. However, some of the newer health professionals were introducing new styles of service delivery. Assertive outreach was being implemented by Northern Birmingham Mental Health Trust, the Care Programme Approach was being adopted by all mental health practitioners and the social model of disability was the preferred model. The Association was sometimes regarded with suspicion for what was regarded as an old-style, outdated model of service delivery.

It soon became clear that one of my most urgent tasks was to convince mental health practitioners and senior managers that the Association had a part to play in the rehabilitation process for mental health service users, that we were committed to the provision of good quality services and that we were prepared to implement the necessary changes to give us the capability to deliver those services. In short, we had to become progressive, dynamic, forward looking, strategic, innovative, professional and much else, and preferably we had to achieve all that as soon as possible.

I needed to provide evidence that industrial therapy could continue to have a very real value for adults with a severe and enduring mental illness by giving them meaningful day time activity that gave them an incentive to get up in the morning. The vision that was promoted was that the Association had a positive approach to mental health, that we had a unique mix of services and support and that industrial therapy should be regarded as a stepping stone on a spectrum towards other activities such as vocational training and open employment.

I was helped in this process by the existence of the Warwick Training Centre which had been set up in 1992. The centre was beginning to develop a reputation for the provision of good quality vocational training delivered in a warm and friendly environment with experienced and qualified tutors. Equally importantly, we were beginning to produce some positive outcomes for students progressing into mainstream education and employment.

One of the first steps I took was to expand the range of training courses by working in partnership with the Economic Development Department to acquire funding from the Further Education Funding Council to deliver training courses that were accredited with a National Vocational Qualification. The first NVQ programmes we offered from September 1996 were Business Administration and Catering & Hospitality. These programmes were added to the existing computer programmes that offered a first level qualification and the pre-vocational training programmes in personal and social development such as confidence building, assertiveness and stress management.

To demonstrate our commitment to innovation the Association had agreed in March 1996 to take part in a project managed by the Economic Development Department and funded by the European Social Fund called the TIME project, TIME being the acronym for Telematics and Mentoring into Employment. Some of the other partners in the TIME project included an independent training provider called ENTA, Bournville College and Kingstanding Adult Education.

From my early days in post the TIME project became a source of both frustration and pride. We were at the cutting edge of technology, using video-conferencing technology when most people had only read about it. For an organisation that did not possess a single computer in March 1996, paid its staff in cash weekly, did its bookkeeping manually in an old fashioned ledger, had no personnel files nor any written policies or procedures, the decision of the Directors to join this innovative project was a leap in the dark and a testament to their commitment to move the organisation into the 21st century.

The technology was duly installed although not without its glitches, students recruited and when we took part in a video conference with the President of the European Parliament, Herr Hanscher, together with Christine Crawley, the Member of the European Parliament for Birmingham, we all glowed with pride at our achievement. The TIME project continued for a further year and many students progressed through the training into mainstream education and employment.

Another project that helped to demonstrate our commitment to innovation was the development of Warwick Candles, our first economic social firm and our subsequent involvement with another European Social Fund project, the Horizon project. The idea behind the concept of the economic social firm was to develop another model of employment opportunities for people with disabilities. A social firm would operate just like any other business but with a cushion of support for trainees who were unable to function at 100% capacity. The objective was to generate sufficient income from the sale of goods or services to create real jobs for people with disabilities.

Our social firm was the result of an idea from Sarah Crawley, a senior officer with the Economic Development Department. Sarah was also a Director of the Association and had been associated with the organisation since the early 1990's when she had worked with us to obtain the funding to set up the Warwick Training Centre. Sarah was also instrumental in persuading Directors to accept the TIME project and now she wanted us to be part of the Horizon project to help us to develop Warwick Candles as a flagship for the organisation. Her ability to secure funding and her enthusiasm for these projects allied to her positive encouragement and support was a key part of the organisation's ability to develop itself during these years.

My first year in post continued with the introduction of a number of new working practices allied to staff training and development. I was determined to develop best practice in the way our services were delivered and this meant our staff had to develop their own awareness and understanding of mental ill health and to be committed to best practice. This was not always easy to achieve. A majority of staff were still employed by Northern Birmingham Mental Health Trust and remained on secondment to the Association. Their terms and conditions varied from Association staff and not surprisingly some tension existed between the two groups. They were responsible to a Trust Manager at All Saints Hospital and only accepted instructions from that direction.

Other introductions designed to benefit the service users included a Carers' Group, an Induction pack for new service users and the development of the existing Users' Group into a more user led body. World Mental Health Day in October of that year was marked by a successful Open Day. We also introduced certificate presentations to mark the achievements of students who had obtained qualifications, many of them the first such they had achieved in their entire life to date. It was always a very special occasion for service users and one which we tried to make important by having one of the Directors to present the certificates in a formal way.

On the basis that the Association was about progression towards work, we also implemented a retirement policy at 70 and held formal retirement presentations for a number of individuals who were aged over 70 and had been with the Association for many years. Indeed one lady was aged 80 and had been at BITA for 30 years!

A word about terminology needs to be inserted here. When the Association was first set up the people who used our services were referred to as 'patients' and indeed this term was used in the original Memorandum and Articles. My background in the voluntary sector had made me more familiar and comfortable with the term 'clients'. This terminology was in keeping with the trend towards consumer led services and the philosophy that services were delivered to clients and that they had a choice in how the service was delivered.

The Memorandum and Articles were changed by Special resolution at the Annual General Meeting the following year in 1997. However, some people within the mental health services felt that the term client implied an unequal relationship and possibly one of patronage. The current trend leans towards a more equal relationship and the term 'service user' and even 'survivor' has become the preferred word. Not everyone felt comfortable with that term but 'service user' has now been adopted by most people working within mental health services.

As my first year in post drew to a close I began to explore various sources of external funding in order to begin the process of developing services away from just industrial therapy and more towards training, vocational advice and employment support. So began a round of submitting funding applications to a range of charitable trusts, the new Lottery Fund, the local authority and the statutory bodies of health and social services.

Our first big grant came from social services in March 1997 from an underspend in the Mental Illness Specific Grant. We had managed to obtain a couple of £1000 donations from local charities , but this time we received a £15000 capital grant to refurbish a disused area of the building on the first floor and create a large training room and a new staff room and toilets. Up until that point male and female staff had taken their breaks in separate rooms! The building work was an important step in developing the Association's work and the grant was a recognition by social services that they valued our work and were prepared to fund its future.

Later in 1997 we were successful in obtaining a grant of £5000 from Lloyds/TSB for a part-time employment support worker. This was to be the first step in the strategy to re-focus the organisation away from merely providing sheltered work to offering service users a progression towards open employment. Towards the end of that year we were also successful with an application to the National Lottery Charities Board and received a 3-year revenue grant for around £64000 for a vocational skills adviser.

From the beginning I had made it a priority of my work to raise the profile of the organisation by networking with a wide range of organisations and individuals within the mental health services both in the statutory and voluntary sector. I knew from my previous work in the voluntary sector that such networking provided opportunities for funding, profile raising and increasingly partnership working. During 1997 I attended conferences and meetings, seminars and task groups. I chaired panel sessions and group discussions. I gave presentations and speeches and was then asked to chair a task group on training and employment set up by Birmingham Health Authority as one of 14 task groups working to produce a Pan-Birmingham Mental Health Strategy. This was an important step as the contacts I made during that work led to our involvement in a project that was to see the Association start its first outreach centre since the car wash was closed.

In September 1997 we held the first public Annual General Meeting for many years, addressed by guest speaker John Mahoney, Chief Executive of Northern Birmingham Mental Health Trust. Since its inception BITA had held close links with All Saints Hospital, where the current Chairman, Dr Norman Imlah had been the last Medical Director before its incorporation into the new NHS structure. John Mahoney was highly regarded for his visionary approach to mental health and it was gratifying to hear him praise the work of the Association.

The St Anne's project was to take up much of my time during 1998. The project was based in East Birmingham, in Saltley, a deprived part of the city which was attracting regeneration money. The project was in partnership with several other agencies, crossing the statutory and voluntary sector. The building was a disused convent owned by Family Housing Association who were expanding their social housing and had agreed with Northern Birmingham Mental Health Trust and Birmingham Social Services a partnership involving a 9-bed residential unit and a day centre on the ground floor. The residential unit was to provide accommodation for patients being discharged from All Saints and Highcroft Hospitals and for clients of Social Services who were ready to move into more independent living.

However, Social Services, having embarked on a review of their day centre provision, decided they did not wish to have another day centre. The project looked as though it might founder and, in order to save its future, the Director of Service Policy and Planning at Northern Birmingham Mental Health Trust, Paul Rooney undertook to underwrite the rent of the ground floor and asked BITA to manage the delivery of a new training and employment service. I put together a bid to Birmingham Health Authority for £274000 of Joint Finance and in March 1998 the bid received initial approval.

That year saw BITA involved in further expansion of its work when South Birmingham Mental Health Trust asked us to operate the refreshment bar to be run by service users at the newly built Longbridge Health and Community Centre. The Centre was an innovative scheme and brought together the delivery of several services run by three Trusts, Acute, Community and Mental Health. The refreshment bar was planned to cement the Centre and turn it from just a Health Centre into a Community Centre. In discussion with the community mental health staff we agreed to deliver two training programmes at the centre, one in Care Skills and one in Food Hygiene to train service users who wanted to work in the refreshment bar.

During all these negotiations and plans to expand our outreach work on both sides of the city, the work at the main Digbeth site continued to be developed. The closure of the Epilepsy Workshop in Edgbaston in July 1998 led to a number of referrals and prompted a reconsideration at Board level of whether such referrals were appropriate within the criteria of our client group and indeed within the Memorandum and Articles. Research revealed no other suitable centres for people with epilepsy. It was finally agreed to take a small number of referrals on a case by case basis for a trial period to assess suitability. Funding was provided individually by social services.

Around this time, the West Midlands Probation Service approached us and asked us to provide places for some of their clients who were resident in a bail hostel that was restricted to people diagnosed with a psychiatric illness. Again a policy decision was required and Directors gave their positive agreement to this partnership with several conditions. Risk assessments had to be provided on each referral and we would not accept referrals for people diagnosed with a severe personality disorder. Funding was to come through the Home Office partnership programme.

In 1998 we held a very successful public event to celebrate the achievements of the trainee workers in Warwick Candles. The business was part of the Social Firms Network and so we had access to a number of services including marketing, publicity and product development. The business was beginning to develop itself with marketing brochures, stands at the NEC Spring Fair and a range of new candles designed to attract sales from retail outlets. The trainees who had been attached to the Warwick Candles workshop had all achieved accredited qualifications. We decided to mark the occasion and invited Roy Hattersley who had retired as MP for Birmingham Sparkbrook the previous year, to present certificates at a Celebration of Achievement. Under the banner of the Social Firms Network which was supported by the Economic Development Department, we also had Councillor Gerard Coyne, the Chair of the Economic Development Committee.

There was a long connection with Roy Hattersley who had been a guest at BITA some 30 years earlier when he was then a Minister of Employment in the 1966-1970 Labour Government. The Chairman was able to produce the original invitation when welcoming Lord Hattersley as he had recently become. The event was well organised and well received by all who attended especially the service users, students and trainees who were delighted to be presented with their certificates by such a well-known figure as Roy Hattersley.

Later that year in September 1998 we held another public occasion when the guest speaker at the Annual General Meeting was Christine Crawley, Member of the European Parliament for Birmingham. She praised our work with various projects made possible by the European Social Fund.

The closing months of 1998 saw the end of an era in terms of the way in which staff were employed within the Association. Since its inception, nursing staff from All Saints Hospital had been seconded to work at BITA. Gradually, as these staff retired, new staff were employed by the Association and the numbers of seconded staff became smaller. The last seconded nurse was Millie Kerley and when she retired the transition from dual management to own management was complete.

Opportunities are there to be grasped and during 1999 an opportunity arose to bid for capital money available in the Single Regeneration Budget to improve premises in areas of regeneration. The Digbeth premises were just within the boundary of one such area. The project was being handled by the Economic Development Department. However, it transpired that we could only receive a percentage of the money needed for the work required and so, an application was made to the National Lottery Charities Board. Architects plans were drawn up and the whole of that year was spent in applications for planning permission and putting together applications for grants to charitable trusts. However, by the end of year we had successfully obtained the whole capital amount of over £60000 and the building refurbishment could proceed.

The St Anne's project had finally come to fruition and in April 1999 the St Anne's Centre opened. The official opening was delayed until June 1999 and when the Lord Mayor, Councillor Ian McCardle cut the ribbon outside the building there was a generally felt sigh of relief that the project had made it to completion. The

Chair of Family Housing Association together with all the other partners paid tribute to the unique partnership work that had taken place to see the project through some difficult moments to its final opening. The newly appointed Chair of the Social Services Committee, Councillor Susannah McCorry was particularly effusive in her praise for this unique partnership and the benefits it could bring in developing best practice.

Delays had occurred for all the usual reasons associated with any building project, but the partnership nature of the project also caused some problems that were only ironed out by countless meetings. Simon Barton, the Social Services Commissioning Manager for Mental Health chaired these meetings and it is to his credit that the meetings were generally good natured and any difficulties were eventually negotiated and essential compromises reached.

Our project on the ground floor was independent from the residential accommodation on the first floor, but we had been involved in the public consultation led by MIND in Birmingham who were managing the accommodation. We had experienced opposition from local residents, sometimes expressed in the unpleasant prejudiced manner that is bred by ignorance and fear of the nature of mental illness and the misconceptions about the sort of people they thought were to be their neighbours. In the event opposition waned when the nature of the scheme was explained.

Our training and employment project centred around a textiles workshop which we planned to develop as a social firm, offering accredited training and work opportunities from the contract work we hoped to obtain for making soft furnishings. We gave it the working name of St Anne's Textiles and in the event, the name stuck and the business remains known by that title. We also planned to offer a range of pre-vocational training programmes similar to those available at Warwick Training Centre. The Joint Finance agreement contained targets we had to reach but we were confident of meeting these as we knew there was substantial unmet need in the area. The joint finance provided for an additional five members of staff to be appointed.

Other developments were proceeding that year and in March 1999 we heard that we had been successful in obtaining £30000 from the Tudor Trust for a 3-year grant towards the salary costs of an Employment Support Worker. We had previously had a part-time worker for 6 months but this had not really begun to deliver anything meaningful and so this grant was the beginning of a real attempt to develop employment support for the service users at BITA.

However, by the middle of 1999 it was becoming clear that the Longbridge Café was not financially viable. Visitors to the Centre were not as high as anticipated and the café was not achieving our objectives of generating enough income to employ any service users. Income was not even covering our own expenditure and losses were beginning to be incurred. Reluctantly the decision was taken withdraw from the project at the end of August 1999. We continued to deliver training programmes however and the relationship with the Trust remained positive, as one of their Service Managers Kate Baylis had recently been elected onto the Board of Directors. It had been a salutary lesson about the difficulties associated with running a catering establishment and impacted on later decisions connected with the building refurbishment at Digbeth.

In September 1999 we held our Annual General Meeting and that year our guest speaker was Philip Hunt, formerly Chief Executive of the National Association of Health Authorities and Trusts, a Labour Peer and then a Government junior Health Minister.

In March 2000 before the building work started we held another event to mark our achievement of the Investors in People award. We had made the decision some three years earlier to work towards this particular standard as we felt it was more relevant than the ISO 9000. There were times during those three years when I felt we would never achieve the standard required. Working with Birmingham and Solihull TEC who provided a consultant to advise us and financial assistance towards staff training, we spent three years working to meet the various quality standards. While the standards were not particularly onerous at first sight, for a small organisation such as BITA with limited resources, it was a major achievement. We invited Dr Jenny Bywaters, Senior Commissioning Manager for Mental Health at Birmingham Health Authority to unveil the plaque and present certificates to all the staff. She had seen the organisation develop over many years and commented that we should be proud of this particular achievement.

The middle part of the year 2000 was largely taken up with building work at the Digbeth site. This was a major project and would take between 8-10 weeks on site. Tenders were put out, architects, quantity surveyors and builders were ever present and all the dust and noise associated with structural building work was to be endured. The original plan to create a sandwich bar had been shelved following the demise of the Longbridge Café. It was felt that the exacting requirements of the food and hygiene legislation were too onerous and an alternative plan for a retail outlet had been agreed. The retail outlet would proved a showcase for products from Warwick Candles and St Anne's Textiles, a facility for the sale of confectionery and soft drinks and a placement opportunity for students on the new Retail NVQ training programme.

The rest of the building work revolved around improvements to the front of the building, a new front door and reception and a new office for the employment support worker. The shop opened in July 2000 and was named 'habitation', with the middle '**bita**' highlighted. We held a grand opening with the Lord Mayor, Councillor Theresa Stewart who unveiled a brass plaque and presented certificates to students as well as acting as the guest speaker at the Annual General Meeting. Councillor Stewart had a long standing association with BITA dating back to the time when she was Chair of the Social Services Committee. She commended the organisation for its services and its willingness to adapt to changing circumstances. The occasion was a high point on the life of the organisation, celebrating as it did this major development for the Association.

However no organisation can afford to rest on its laurels and I was always looking for opportunities to develop in other directions. While the key objective remained to expand the availability of the employment support service, other services always carried value for the service users. The National Lottery Charities Board was always a good source of funding. We had been remarkably successful over the last 3 years in achieving both a revenue and a capital grant.

On this occasion the inspiration for the application came from one of the Directors, Alison Coates who was a mental health lecturer on the Nursing Degree course at the University of Birmingham. Alison was a psychiatric nurse by training and background and she was a valuable director in many ways acting as Chair of the Personnel Sub-Committee and always being available for advice and support. She came across a piece of research linking poor mental health with poor physical health and suggested that we should apply for funding for a project. Alison provided me with much of the evidence needed to formulate an application for a Healthy Living Project.

The project's objective was to improve the physical health of mental health service users by means of diet, nutrition and exercise. It was somewhat unaligned from the core activity of the organisation but we felt it could add to the quality of life of the service users. We also decided to submit another application at this time for a User Involvement Worker. I did not entertain very high hopes of success on this occasion as I felt we might have been too ambitious submitting two applications, and so I was probably the most surprised when both applications were successful and we had two more posts to add to the staff establishment from October 2001.

During 2001 we began work with the Information, Advice and Guidance Network, part of the Careers and Education Business Partnership. We received a grant of £10000 to provide vocational advice and guidance to people who were experiencing mental ill health, on this occasion targeting 18-25 year olds. It was to be the beginning of a partnership which is still continuing. It is a valuable part of the organisation's work and because there is a required standard of service, the charter mark is there for everyone to see.

Towards the end of 2001 we became sub-contractors to Economic Development to deliver a job broker programme under the Government scheme New Deal for Disabled People. The contract provided resources to expand the employment support work by appointing another employment support worker on a part-time basis. The following year that work was expanded still further by a successful application to the Neighbourhood Renewal Fund which allowed us to appoint a full time employment support worker based at the St Anne's centre.

I had always wanted to undertake a strategic review of the organisation and had felt for some time that this work had been long overdue. Something else always seemed to come along and this important piece of work kept being delayed. I needed someone or something to provide the impetus and in July 2001 I was introduced to a management consultant who was to fill just that role. David Hall was an engineer by profession and had worked in industry for many years in the Birmingham area before becoming Chief Executive of a TEC. He also happened to be the Chair of MIND in Darlington where he now lived. David had a perfect combination of skills and interests and he prepared terms of reference for the process of a strategic review which the Directors endorsed.

The process recommended by David Hall commenced with a consultation exercise to be carried out with key external stakeholders and it provided the opportunity to meet with senior managers in both Mental Health Trusts, Birmingham Health Authority, Social Services and Economic Development at a time of great change with the imminent move to Primary Care Trusts. The consultation exercise enabled us to discover the views of these key stakeholders about the role of BITA and the future of any partnership work. David prepared reports from all these meetings which were fed back to the Directors. The consultation exercise continued with internal consultation with staff and Directors at separate Away Days in December 2001 and January 2002.

Unfortunately the process of the strategic review had to be temporarily halted in March 2002 when a most unwelcome crisis hit the organisation following the decision by Social Services to cease their funding of the St Anne's Centre. The Joint Finance agreement expired in March 2002 and we had spent the previous 12 months attempting to put together a combination of partners to replace the funding needed to run the St Anne's Centre. Birmingham Health Authority had agreed to contribute 50% of the revenue costs, to be rolled over into the new Memorandum of Agreement with the Primary Care Trust, but Social Services had delayed their decision until the last moment and we were now faced with a huge hole in the finances.

An emergency Finance Committee was called and despite much juggling of the figures, it proved impossible to set a balanced budget. Under the Charity Commission rules we were not allowed to agree a deficit budget and the Directors were forced to issue a closure notice on the St Anne's centre and redundancy notices on all the nine members of staff. I had three months in which to find a solution to this crisis. That period was probably one of the most difficult times I had experienced at BITA. Apart from the potential loss of the service, most of the staff at the St Anne's Centre were service users as we had tried to put into practice our commitment to employment of service users. I felt an acute sense of responsibility for the situation and was determined to find a rescue plan.

I embarked upon a round of meetings and negotiations with any potential funding sources. I managed to persuade Family Housing Association to waive the rent for the first quarter of the financial year and arranged meetings with Social Services and the newly formed East Birmingham Primary Care Trust in whose catchment area the St Anne's Centre was located. Social Services remained unable to assist; they were in the throes of their own financial crisis.

However, the new Chief Executive of the East Birmingham Primary Care Trust, Sophia Christie had the foresight to recognise that the St Anne's Centre was providing a valuable service to local residents and that it would be at tragedy if it had to close. She agreed to meet the required shortfall. With just three weeks to spare the Directors were presented with a revised budget and agreed to lift the closure notice and rescind the redundancy notices. It had been a very difficult time for the organisation.

The work around the strategic review re-commenced in June, after a three month delay but the work progressed well and by the end of the year I was able to present a draft strategic plan to the Board of Directors for approval. The plan proposed that the organisation should re-affirm its mission statement and focus our work around the provision of pathways to employment, while recognising that not all mental health service users were able to obtain employment, but that we could encourage progression towards employment by small stepping stones along the way.

In December 2002 we were greatly saddened to learn that one of our Directors Billy Ko had died suddenly. He had been a great supporter of BITA and was very popular with the many service users who knew him well. It had been his suggestion, at one of the Directors' Away Days, that we should give our new strategic plan the title 'Pathways to Employment' and he will be remembered for that thoughtful contribution.

So in January 2003 we entered our 40th Anniversary year with a Strategic Plan and an organisation looking forward to remaining dynamic and positive, well placed to continue delivering good quality services and being positive about mental health.

Chapter Twelve

CONCLUSION

This chapter concludes the history of the first forty years of BITA. When the continuation of its embryonic existence required me to say I would support its modest beginnings there was no crystal ball to foretell this history forty years on. At that time it was one expedient, among a number, to try to deal with serious hospital overcrowding, and finding ways of safely returning a proportion of the institutionalised hospital population to the unreceptive community outside. When one plants seeds there is no way of telling which will flower, and which will wither away.

At that time also there was no thought that the large psychiatric hospitals which had been around for a hundred years would disappear within the next forty years. Yet the seeds of their departure were sown in that decade of the mid-fifties to mid-sixties. In the beginning we moved cautiously, very aware of the need to take time and trouble to prepare people for their return to the community by ensuring their stability and making them self-reliant. Equally there was an awareness of the need to prepare the community to accept and tolerate those people who were returning. For a hundred years they had been swept away into large institutions, largely isolated, out of sight, and outcasts from society. So in the beginning to ease them back we began to create halfway houses, day care centres, and the workshops for rehabilitation. After that came the creation of community nurses to manage the steadily increasing numbers living outside hospital, but still under treatment.

For about twenty years this process went along, carefully evolving the transition to care in the community. In some places, and in some hospitals this process took place earlier, and more rapidly, than in others, with enterprising innovations depending very much on local initiatives. In those twenty years most of the people with the best chance of making a safe and acceptable return to the community did so, even though a proportion had to return periodically for further treatment in hospital.

Eventually each large hospital was left with a rump of patients who were too elderly, or too chronically damaged to make the transition to the community without greatly increased community resources to back the new initiatives. It was at this point that community care began to break down. Politicians and government officials pressed administrators to put plans in operation for a rapid rundown of the remaining hospital populations prior to an early closure of those hospitals. This policy did not take into account two fundamental problems. The first was the very dependent nature of the remaining patients in hospital compared to those that had already been rehabilitated. The second, and more important, is the failure to acknowledge that caring for people with those greater handicaps in the community would require far more resources in carers, and in costs, than was provided for them in the institutions, and that provision was not made beforehand, or even at the time. Unhappily community care came into disrepute, and is still trying to recover.

Today health administrators and professionals are still repairing the damage caused by the poorly planned and under financed final phase of the old psychiatric hospitals. They have an uphill task as public confidence remains low, and resources to provide carers and other facilities still get a low priority in overall health budgets. In addition there remains a shortage of acute beds, despite the creation of various small units around the community. It results in many leaving hospital before they are sufficiently stable, and this is one of the problems we face in rehabilitation today. The relative isolation of these smaller units does tend to limit the range of services they offer, compared with those that were available in larger hospitals. While nobody wishes to see a return to the institutions of old, had they been allowed to fade away more gradually, and with more foresight, many of the distresses that have occurred in recent years might have been avoided.

It is also worth reflecting, when planning for the future, that after the appearance of a range of revolutionary drugs for the treatment of major illnesses such as schizophrenia and affective psychosis in the 1950s and 1960s there has been relatively little advance in more specific treatment for these illnesses. Although new products have appeared bringing possible marginal refinements, and sometimes only arguably better, as with more recent anti-depressants, there has been no fundamental breakthrough in treatment for nearly fifty years, and specific causation or cure has yet to be found. Moreover these illnesses may be getting more prevalent. There are increasing reports that the widespread abuse of drugs such as cannabis may be acting as a precipitant of schizophrenia in young vulnerable adults, something that many in clinical practice have been aware of for some time. Like many observations and findings it is not new, only rediscovered. Over a hundred years ago the Medical Director of a psychiatric hospital in Cairo attributed the high rate of mental breakdown in male patients, as compared with female, to their widespread use of hashish.

History is full of truths being rediscovered. Our approach and philosophy is not new. Over a hundred years ago humane administrators in this city, in our defunct institutions, were advocating work and recreation as therapeutic. If we define these as meaningful activity it is a maxim that should not be forgotten, but too often it is neglected, even today, when one finds far too many people discharged with little thought given to how they will spend their day. All too often it is forgotten that occupation is important for well-being and self-esteem whereas idleness is soul destroying and destructive. Community care in itself does not solve the problems of isolation, apathy and withdrawal which can occur just as much in the community as they did in the institution.

The industrial therapy pioneers of forty-fifty years ago gave the concept of work as a therapeutic requirement some renewed meaning. In some places their original initiatives have disappeared and not been replaced. In Birmingham, at BITA, we try to keep it alive but we can only do so by adapting our basic beliefs in an ever-changing world. A favourite Scottish author, Grassic Gibbon, once wrote that nothing is true but change.

This is a record of our history over the past forty years. We continue to plan for the future. Our immediate objectives are to continue to offer training opportunities and rehabilitative facilities to those in need, mindful that we must evolve and adapt to changing requirements. At the same time we must never forget our fundamental aims, or lose sight of the lessons we have learned over the last forty years.

Appendix

BOARD OF DIRECTORS

Dr Norman Imlah	
Chair	Retired Consultant Psychiatrist, last Medical Director All Saints Hospital
Peter Townley	Business Development Consultant
Dr Alan Ogden	Retired Consultant Psychiatrist
Dr Tom Harrison	Consultant Psychiatrist South Birmingham Mental Health Trust
Sarah Crawley	Social Firms UK Chair, funding consultant
Kate Baylis	Service Manager, South Birmingham Mental Health Trust
Alison Coates	Lecturer in mental health nursing, University of Birmingham
Peter Imlah	Service Manager, North Birmingham Mental Health Trust
James Cody	Retired Community Psychiatric Nurse

Observers

Peter Beddard	Management Accountant, Arundale & Co
Susan Downes	Disability Development Officer, Birmingham City Council
Julie Richmond	External Funding Director, South Birmingham College

About the Author

Dr. Norman Imlah is Chairman of The Birmingham Industrial Therapy Association a charity which provides workshops and training for psychiatric patients. He has a long and distinguished career in the field of psychiatry with particular reference to the study and treatment of patients recovering from drug addiction.

For many years he was Medical Director of All Saints Hospital Birmingham, he is also a past Chairman of the Birmingham Branch of The British Medical Association.

Dr Imlah is the author of a number of authoritative texts on psychiatry.

By the Same Author